WHO'S WHO of the BRAIN

of related interest

The Complete Guide to Asperger's Syndrome
Tony Attwood
ISBN 978 1 84310 495 7 (Hardback)
ISBN 978 1 84310 669 2 (Paperback)
eISBN 978 1 84642 559 2

Freaks, Geeks and Asperger Syndrome
A User Guide to Adolescence
Luke Jackson
Foreword by Tony Attwood
ISBN 978 1 84310 098 0
eISBN 978 1 84642 356 7

The Man who Lost his Language
A Case of Aphasia: Revised Edition
Sheila Hale
ISBN 978 1 84310 564 0
eISBN 978 1 84642 626 1

Stroke Survivor
A Personal Guide to Recovery
Andy McCann
Forewords by Robin Sieger and The Stroke Association
ISBN 978 1 84310 410 0
eISBN 978 1 84642 472 4

Touch and Go Joe
An Adolescent's Experience of OCD
Joe Wells
Foreword by Isobel Heyman
ISBN 978 1 84310 391 2
eISBN 978 1 84642 489 2

WHO'S WHO of the BRAIN

A Guide to Its Inhabitants, Where they Live and What they Do

Kenneth Nunn, Tanya Hanstock and Bryan Lask

Illustrated by Linn Iril Hjelseth
Brain diagrams by Edward Clayton

Jessica Kingsley *Publishers*
London and Philadelphia

First published in 2008
by Jessica Kingsley Publishers
116 Pentonville Road
London N1 9JB, UK
and
400 Market Street, Suite 400
Philadelphia, PA 19106, USA

www.jkp.com

Library of Congress Cataloging in Publication Data
Nunn, Kenneth P.
    Who's who of the brain : a guide to its inhabitants, where they live and what they do /
Kenneth Nunn, Tanya Hanstock and Bryan Lask.
        p. cm.
    Includes index.
    ISBN 978-1-84310-470-4 (pb : alk. paper) 1. Brain--Popular works. I. Hanstock, Tanya.
II. Lask, Bryan. III. Title.
    QP376.N856 2008
    612.8--dc22
                                                      2007047560

British Library Cataloguing in Publication Data
A CIP catalogue record for this book is available from the British Library

ISBN 978 1 84310 470 4
eISBN 978 1 84642 798 5

Printed and bound in Great Britain

Kenneth dedicates this book to Rhonda, his wife
and lifelong friend.

Tanya dedicates this book to her partner, Ed, a fellow neuroscience
enthusiast, who has provided great company and support.

Bryan dedicates this book to Aaron Lask, his father and inspiration,
and to Raffi Arthur Aaron Lask, his grandson
and new guiding light.

Contents

Part Three: The Subcortex

Part Four: The Brain Stem, Cerebellum and Beyond

Part Five: The Community as a Whole

Acknowledgements

Kenneth

I thank all my colleagues at the Nexus Unit at the John Hunter Hospital in Newcastle, New South Wales, for their support and encouragement at the weekly Brain Breakfast meetings and my colleagues at the Children's Hospital Westmead for their encouragement by supporting the weekly Neuroscientific Aspects of Psychiatry Meeting for more than a decade. I want especially to thank Associate Professor Janice Muir, and Dr Ruth Urwin, Senior Hospital Scientist in Molecular Neuropsychiatry, for their collegiate understanding and support during the last five years on all matters molecular, neuroscientific and psychiatric. I am particularly appreciative of my colleagues in CAMHSNET (now MH-Kids) in New South Wales, who have supported me more than can be imagined, through all 'the slings and arrows' of modern health systems, especially Dr Adrian Falkov. I would like to thank Professor Philip Graham, who first started me on the road to the developing brain, my colleagues at St George's University of London Eating Disorder Research Team, and the RASP research team in Oslo, where I spent three months pulling together many of my ideas. To Professor Beverley Raphael goes my longest academic mentorship reaching back now for 30 years.

Tanya

First and foremost I thank my coauthors for their unique skills and talents that they have brought to this book and for teaching me a great deal along the way. Thank you to Edward Clayton for assisting with a wide range of activities from proof reading to helping with the drawing of the brain diagrams. Thank you to Dr Ria Leonard for expert proofreading. Thank you to Paul Mallet who first got me addicted to neuroscience. My inspiration for this book came from the inaugural Brain Breakfast programme and I would particularly like to thank those who regularly presented and helped organise these weekly neuroscience meetings: Kenneth Nunn, Sally Hunt, Jenny Geddes, Lee Sturgeon, Jeannette Walsh, Teri Stone, Edward Clayton, Philip Hazell, Colin Kable, Jude Payling, David Burton, Lawrence Dadd and Fiona Dezalak. Thank you to the team at The Bipolar Program and the Psychological Assistance Service; particularly Stephen Hirneth, Colin Kable, Sean Halpin and Erika Giegerl, for creating a stimulating and enjoyable work environment. I thank my family, friends and colleagues, and rats 5 and 6, for their support and encouragement. I thank my clients who teach me about mental health, how the brain works and better ways to explain this to others. Finally I thank great authors such as James Kalat, Michael Gazzaniga and Rita Carter for their brilliant books we have referenced and who have also provided inspiration for us to write our own book.

Bryan

I am so grateful to Isky Gordon, whose friendship and determination led me into the realm of neuroscience; also to many other colleagues at Great Ormond Street Hospital for Children, and later at St George's University of London, who joined or encouraged me in my first faltering steps, and especially Beth Watkins and Ian Frampton for tolerating and guiding me. A heartfelt thank you to so many colleagues at the Regional Eating Disorders Service, Ulleval University Hospital, Oslo, and especially Trine Wiig, who all provided so much invaluable support and friendship during a particularly difficult time for me in the six months before completion of this book. You guys will never know how much that meant to me. A very warm thank you to Rachel Bryant-Waugh, who has always been such a wonderful friend and inspiring colleague. Thank you so much to Eirin Winje for her enthusiastic support, advice and friendship during the writing of this book, and most especially for introducing us to our brilliant illustrator, Linn Iril Hjelseth. And, thank you, Ana.

And finally a very warm acknowledgement from us all to Dylan Thomas and *Under Milk Wood*.

Preface

The human brain has been described as the most complex structure in the universe, so complex that it is beyond the ability of the human brain to understand. This book is written, more than a little ambitiously, in an attempt to achieve the seemingly impossible. It is perhaps a little arrogant of us to hold out hope that in less than 300 pages we can make sense of the mysterious workings of 100 billion neurons (nerve cells) and the one thousand connections for each such cell (making 100 trillion connections). And we won't even do more than mention in passing that each neuron is supported by glial cells of which there are more than 100 billion!

We hope that what follows will offer at least some understanding for those who know little or nothing of the workings of the brain, who find the brain a complete, inaccessible, and somewhat frightening mystery. We also hope that those who do have some familiarity with the brain and its functions, whatever their professional background, will gain more knowledge and further insights into how to apply such awareness in everyday clinical practice. As for those already expert in this area, we hope they will enjoy our conceptualisation of this most fascinating of structures, and perhaps make use of it in their teachings to those less knowledgeable than themselves.

Leon Eisenberg said that we are in danger of having a mindless neurology and a brainless psychiatry. Put another way, there is often a failure to link the many structures of the brain with their different and often multiple and overlapping functions in a manner that can be clearly understood. We try to address this dilemma by attempting to merge structure and function, by integrating information from the neuro-scientific revolution with the subtleties of experiential understanding, bringing the two professional fields together. Thus we aim to introduce the brain with the goals of being simultaneously both more scientific and more humanistic.

The book is set in a metaphorical community known as 'Cephalton-upon-Ridge', popularly known by its inhabitants as just 'Cephalton'. The countryside below the Ridge is known as the 'Shire', which in turn is surrounded by an ocean, separating this unique land from the rest of the world. The fascinating community of Cephalton, some parts of it dating back to time immemorial, is populated by a wide variety of complex and colourful characters, each serving his or her own vital function, but each forming part of a highly sophisticated and well-functioning society.

The first chapter describes the geography of Cephalton and introduces each of the key characters within the community. Succeeding chapters focus on each key character in turn, describing who they are and where they live, their personalities, their strengths and weaknesses, their friendships and their functions within Cephalton, and what happens when each is unwell or indisposed. The final chapter shows how they all work together as a tightly knit and well-functioning community, as well as offering a description of one memorable evening in the life of Cephalton when not all went as smoothly as usual.

The allegory of Cephalton and its inhabitants is explained in as clear language as possible. Some technical language is used where absolutely necessary, but a glossary is provided to assist the reader. For some very intriguing or important aspects of Cephalton life, those that are too complex to explain in simple language, a 'technical corner' is provided, allowing readers to pause a while and delve, or simply to bypass, as they so choose. A series of case studies and historical vignettes are provided to highlight the importance of the specific structures under consideration.

While all the parts of the brain are important, we attempt to demonstrate that the most significant aspect is the way in which the brain acts as an integrated system. It enables its owner to live and love, to give and take, to think and feel, to work and play and to adapt in a changing and often challenging world. We hope that readers will find this book as interesting and enjoyable to read as we have experienced in writing it.

Kenneth Nunn, Tanya Hanstock and Bryan Lask

Part One

A Community Called Cephalton-upon-Ridge

Chapter 1

Introducing the Community and Characters of Cephalton-upon-Ridge

Cropped in rock of brown and grey,
lurching to life with light of day,
pinch in an hour glass between the sands,
the inner and the outer lands.
This tiny town of tangled byways
is meeting place for super highways.
Highways to and highways from
a town that points to what's beyond.
Land within only half discovered
Land outside by which all are mothered.

Perched precariously atop a mountain range in a remote land is a small country town called Cephalton-upon-Ridge and its community of somewhat rustic, but always colourful, characters. In satellite snapshots from outer space the casual observer might be forgiven for mistaking the town for a giant walnut in an asteroid crater. The town is surrounded by a land of rolling hills and plains on either side of the great dividing range called the Somite Mountains. These mountains extend from the town like a long tail. The town stands on the highest point of the mountain range looking down on the coast, which like a skin separates the outside world from the inland regions that constitute Cephalton and the Shire.

Cephalton sits astride the meeting place of at least five major highways that come from the Shire to meet in the middle of the great inland lakes and canals. These five major, multi-lane, rapid transit super-highways allow traffic into the town from the Shire. Four separate, more convoluted road systems allow internal traffic out of Cephalton. Traffic travels in only one direction on all roads to avoid accidents and reduce traffic flow problems.

Although there are large mountain lakes and canals in Cephalton, fresh water is pumped up to Cephalton from the Shire. It is distributed via two main pipelines to the North. The Northern, or Watershed, pipelines are by far the biggest distribution system. The two to the south of Cephalton, the Somite pipelines, though smaller, are critical for providing water to the power station in Downtown Cephalton, which enables the survival of the whole Shire and all of Cephalton.

On closer inspection, the town appears to be messy, with lanes and alleys running every which way. This indeed reflects the chequered history of the cycles of growth, decline and struggle for survival of this tiny town of several hundred souls. Still closer examination reveals an orderliness and practicality that inspires admiration in all who visit and get to know its highways and byways and the people who inhabit this craggy lair.

Cephalton has had settlements on the same site dating back for thousands of years with remains and relics still to be found in the Downtown area. This part of town is still referred to by some as Old Cephalton. The modern town was established in what is now known as Midtown Cephalton or Cephalton Proper, and in very recent times expansion into the more gentrified northern suburbs of Uptown Cephalton (also referred to as New Cephalton) has been extensive.

The neighbourhoods in which the town's people live are also well organised, even though to outsiders they appear chaotic and muddled.

The streets, though bending and winding, first this way and then that, are ordered from North to South and from East to West, as well as in Uptown, Midtown and Downtown. Houses are built to merge into the shape of surrounding rocks and idiosyncratic design is standard.

Within each main neighbourhood the location of each person enables them to have quick communication with their closest neighbours. Yet, they can also have contact with those neighbours who are at the other end of town, due to its compact nature and its excellent phone and internet service. Cephalton and the Shire were among the first communities to get the internet and, for a small community, it is quite surprising how many providers of internet services there are, most of which are located in Downtown Cephalton.

There is always something happening in Cephalton. Gossip is much valued here, even when the accuracy of each tale is wanting. The sterile, factual news of more sophisticated communities is thought to be rather pretentious and stand-offish. Only those from Uptown Cephalton greet gossip with the suspicious opprobrium of metropolitan populations. The people in the town have their own unique history and the local historical society flourishes. Every character in the town is worth getting to know in their own right. However, the real strength and depth of characters are best observed as the whole town works together.

Today in Cephalton is much as any other day as the sun rises on the usual cycle of business from the quiet activity of night workers coming off shift work through to the bustling retail periods of the day. Successive waves of people wake up at different times to go about their jobs and lives. The town has people of all shapes and sizes, professions and trades, habits and lifestyles. In one sense it is like any one of a hundred similar country towns. But Cephalton has developed uniquely because of its location and its extraordinary communication system. Its residents are even better informed about what is happening in metropolitan and coastal life than they are about the much slower, less accessible inland of the Shire and the nooks and crannies of Cephalton itself.

'Dramatis personae' – the Cephalton characters and their analogous brain structures

Now is the time to meet some of the key characters in Cephalton-upon-Ridge. First we offer a 'dramatis personae', followed by a simple explanation of the brain itself. In succeeding chapters we will offer an in-depth meeting with each of the key characters and their analogous brain structures.

Uptown residents

Fredrick Foresight: frontal lobes – town mayor and true leader of Cephalton and the Shire and partner to Rochelle. Responsible for executive function in the brain.

Rochelle Ringbond: cingulate gyrus – part of the leadership team of Cephalton and the Shire and partner to Fredrick. Responsible for the supervisory attentional systems and sustained concentration.

Dudley Doit: motor cortex – also part of the leadership team of the town and Shire, partner to Cherry Chatterley. Responsible for the initiating commands of motor activity.

Cherry Chatterley: Broca's area – main news reader, Cherry is partner to Dudley Doit and twin sister to Charles Chatterley. Responsible for communication and sending information.

Charles Chatterley: Wernicke's area – chief telephonist and amateur lexicographer. Responsible for communication, receiving, making sense of information and finding words to give to objects and experiences.

Melissa Mirrorwood: somatosensory cortex – leading gymnast and personal trainer, partner to Maurice Mapply. Responsible for the representation of the body, pain and the perception of body image.

Maurice Mapply: parietal lobes – major land holder, mathematician and lover of Melissa Mirrorwood, maps and all things environmental. Responsible for the representation of the environment, quantifying our experience and attending to spatial details.

Penelope Panorama: occipital lobes – artist and collector of fine art and secret admirer of Maurice Mapply. Responsible for the receiving, organising and dissemination of all things visual.

Lilly Listentale: temporal lobes – archivist at the Cephalton Conservatorium and Dramatic Arts, good friend of Felicity Feelall. Responsible for the receiving, organising and dissemination of all things auditory and the integration of visual, auditory and spatial information, especially faces.

Brenda Bridgehead: insula – Cephalton's richest landowner, philanthropist, influential networker and partner to Dr Ernie Enkephalin. Responsible for linking bodily experience, thinking and emotional experience. This linkage is seen most clearly in the verbal and non-verbal components of communication.

Midtown residents

Christopher Crosstalk: corpus callosum – the 'gentle giant' of Cephalton, whose property joins Eastern and Western Cephalton, keeping both towns in touch with each other. Responsible for communication between both halves of the brain, allowing a greater degree of regional specialisation and duplication simultaneously.

Sage Seahorse: hippocampus – President of the Historical Society, lover of the very passionate Annie Almond and favourite nephew and sole heir to Al Zheimer. Responsible for conscious, personal and contextual memory.

Annie Almond: amygdala – provides an ongoing risk assessment for the whole town, detecting threats and raising the alarm so that her friends Uma Underbride, Horace Hormone and Rosie Reaction can mobilise the whole community. She is also the partner of Sage Seahorse. Responsible for setting off the cascade of responses to threats and stress.

Priscilla Prizeman: nucleus accumbens – Priscilla is a shrewd business woman, intimate friend to Olivia Orgasmia and muse to Fredrick Foresight. She has her own advertising business and casino and is responsible for rewarding and reinforcement of the desirable and providing drive and motivation.

Olivia Orgasmia: septal nuclei – a colourful but enigmatic socialite, lives on Priscilla's estate. Specialises in extremes of pleasure and, in certain circumstances, also rage.

Corrie O'Graphie: basal ganglia – world famous dancer and partner to Frank Finesse. Responsible for implementing movement routines, remembering skills and maintaining muscle tone.

Felicity Feelall: thalamus – sensory therapist and the 'Bosom of Cephalton'. Responsible for filtering, focusing and relaying pain and other sensations to the cortex and subcortex.

Uma Underbride and Horace Hormone: hypothalamus and pituitary – Uma is head of the Emergency services and Horace is the Cephalton pharmacist. They are a very tight knit couple. Responsible for emergency responses to threat, maintenance of homeostasis (stability) and growth and reproduction.

Downtown residents

Fay Faceandear and Sam Swallowtalk: pons and medulla – Fay is 'the face and ears of Cephalton'. She owns the Narrow Bridge Café, the main internet café in Downtown, the conduit for much news about what is happening in Cephalton and the Shire. She is responsible for relaying sensation from the body to the thalamus and messages from the cortex to the body. Sam Swallowtalk is the Director of the Cephalton Power Station and husband of Fay. He is responsible for regulating such basic functions as heart rate, breathing, sleep and waking, and pain control.

Frank Finesse: cerebellum – a world class dancer like his intimate friend, Corrie O'Graphie, and lover of clocks and music. Responsible for coordination, fine tuning and timing of movement and balance.

Rosie Reaction: autonomic nervous system – Rosie is part of the emergency response team, including her sometime lover, Tony Turnon, but also part of the large network of those who are more conservative and like things to stay the same. Responsible for emergency responses of fright, fight and flight, and conservation responses of calming, resting and digesting.

THE DOWNTOWN DREAM TEAM: RETICULAR FORMATION

The dream team contains many important members of the Cephalton community:

Dr Ernie Enkephalin: periaqueductal grey matter – general practitioner, pain specialist and partner to Brenda Bridgehead and colleague of Dr Raffi Restogen. Responsible for pain regulation.

Tony Turnon: locus coeruleus – air-traffic controller part-time emergency worker and sometime lover of Rosie Reaction. Responsible for alertness.

Dr Raffi Restogen: raphe nuclei – specialist in anaesthetics and sleep, colleague of Dr Enkephalin. Responsible for regulating mood, reducing pain and sleep initiating.

Al Zheimer: nucleus of Meynert – philanthropist and pharmaceutical baron. Responsible for arousal and memory.

Tim Tickertaste: nucleus solitarius – eccentric engineer, author of the Cephalton 'Good Food Guide' and favourite bachelor uncle to Rosie Reaction. Responsible for respiratory regulation, blood pressure regulation and registration of danger in food.

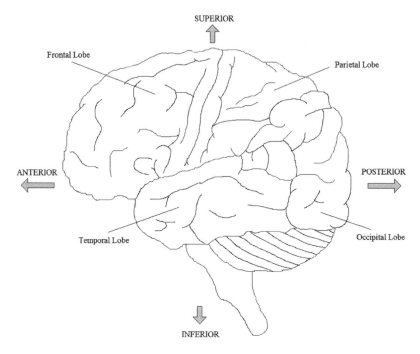

Figure 1.1. Lateral view (outer surface) of the left side of the brain showing four main orientation positions shaded in grey. Each of the main visible lobes of the brain is labelled.

The brain – an introduction

The brain has evolved over hundreds of millions of years to be a very complex collection or community of structures. Each part of the brain has specialised functions but all parts work in unison to help us adapt to and survive in our environment. Brain structures are the same between different people, different cultures and different environments.

Location, structure and function

The brain is organised along at least three different dimensions:

1. *Anterior–posterior* – roughly speaking this means from the front to the back of the head, corresponding to North to South in Cephalton. The more anterior structures tend to be

involved with personality, speech, initiative and emotion, whilst the more posterior ones tend to be involved with sensation, perception and automatic regulation. Three large spaces within the cranium lie along this anterior–posterior axis: the *anterior fossa* (or cave) which is largely filled with frontal lobes, the *middle fossa* which has the bulk of the brain including the parietal, temporal and occipital lobes, and the *posterior fossa* which contains the brain stem and cerebellum.

2.   *Right–left* – this lateral perspective, corresponding to East and West in Cephalton, distinguishes between the two halves of the brain. The right hemisphere is more involved with space, place, attention and emotions and the left with time, rules, sequencing, logic, meaning and speech.

3.   *Cortical and subcortical* – the *cortex* or outer layer of the brain (Uptown Cephalton) is made up of grey matter, which consists of densely packed nerve fibres (the word cortex comes from the Latin word for the bark of a tree). The layer beneath the cortex is called the *subcortex* and consists mainly of white matter. These are nerve fibres, covered by layers of fat known as myelin, which connect different parts of the brain. The myelin provides insulation to prevent misfiring and miscommunication when winding through the depths of the brain and allows for rapid transfer of information. Cortical structures are involved with perception, awareness, conscious thought and memory, analysis, decision-making, speech and deliberate movement. Subcortical structures above the brain stem are involved with unconscious processes, including emotional regulation, unconscious memory, automatic movement, hormonal and temperature regulation. The lower subcortical structures, at the level of the brain stem, are involved in arousal (consciousness and sleep), facial sensation and movement, and regulation of breathing, heart rate and ingestion of food.

The brain communicates within and outside of itself via a highly elaborate combination of chemical messengers and nerve fibre links that provide an almost infinite array of possible messages. There are over a hundred different chemicals providing 100 billion (10^{11}) neurons, with 100 (10^{14}) trillion connections or synapses. These enable sensation to be received, perceived, integrated and interpreted and motor activity to be initiated and maintained.

There are two main arterial systems providing the brain with blood and therefore oxygen and nutrients: the *carotid system* supplying the front two-thirds of the brain (anterior and middle cerebral arteries) and the *vertebral system* supplying the back and base of the brain (posterior cerebral artery and basilar arteries). The carotid system supports all of the higher functions of the brain while the vertebral system supports all of the vital functions.

Connections

Connections may be broadly divided into sensory and motor.

SENSORY CONNECTIONS

There are five channels or systems of sensory information entering from the outside world: taste, touch, smell, hearing and vision. Taste and smell – the chemical senses – are relatively less developed in humans compared to many other animal species. The senses are all drawn together in the thalamus, a structure at the very centre of the brain.

MOTOR CONNECTIONS

There are four channels or systems for providing output or motor function:

1. *The pyramidal system* – this deals with voluntary motor activity. It is so called because at the point in its pathways where many of the fibres from each side of the brain cross over to

the other side of the body, the shape of the fibre tracts resembles, to the imaginative eye, pyramids.

2.   *The extrapyramidal system* – a motor system outside the pyramidal tract provides the pre-packaged action patterns that make the full action sequences of daily life possible.

3.   *The cerebellar system* – this finesses all motor activity to make it a smooth, sequenced and precision movement.

4.   *The autonomic nervous system* – enables muscles to move in a crisis with the flight or fight response, and controls movements that occur throughout our inner organs, such as the gut.

The essence of brain activity is its complex interconnectedness. Although the brain looks chaotic and at times rather random, it is in fact highly organised. The connections are vital in the way we experience our two worlds: the world of the external environment which is 'mother to us all' and the inner world of our conscious and unconscious life.

Although most of the time the brain functions smoothly, efficiently and effectively, from time to time things can go wrong. These include:

*   genetically determined conditions, such as chromosomal abnor-malities

*   pre- and perinatal events which can have a profound effect on the highly vulnerable developing brain

*   a wide range of brain pathologies at any time during life, such as: infections (e.g. meningitis or encephalitis); trauma due to head injury; metabolic or neurotransmitter upheaval; cerebrovascular disease leading to ischaemia, infarctions, haemorrhages, emboli or aneurysms; seizures due to excessively intense and/or syn-chronised activity of cortical neurones; neurodegenerative disorders such as Alzheimer's disease, Huntington's disease, Parkinson's disease or motor neurone disease; demyelination disorders such as multiple sclerosis in which there is scarring and a loss of nerve axons; and neoplasms (tumours and cancers)

Conclusion

And so the scene is set to explore Cephalton and meet its inhabitants. We start in Uptown Cephalton, the newest part of town, where the intellectuals tend to gather, where thought is of the essence, where plans and decisions are made and action initiated. Later we will travel to Midtown Cephalton and meet the characters involved with what might be considered the automatic and emotional aspects of community life, and then Downtown where we will meet those central to some of the most vital aspects of community life, the 'heart and lungs' of Cephalton. We welcome you to Cephalton-upon-Ridge and hope you enjoy your visit.

Part Two

The Cerebral Cortex

Chapter 2

Fredrick Foresight: the Frontal Lobes

Meet Fredrick Foresight

In Uptown Cephalton there is a compact but internally spacious house owned by Fredrick Foresight and his partner Rochelle Ringbond. From their house there is a panoramic view of the whole town. As a couple they are young, dynamic and take a lead role in whatever is preoccupying or dominating town affairs.

Fredrick is the key person in the community. Although he is the youngest member of the town council, he is the most capable, and unless he gives the OK, nothing goes ahead. Almost every part of the town's identity has his distinct stamp. He is the ultimate big picture person. Although Fredrick is often the last to arrive in any crisis, he is usually the one who saw it coming. He is known for his capacity to keep abreast of what is happening throughout the town and for his cool, hard logic when needed. He listens to the 'demons and the angels' of town life but always tries to see for himself – and to help others to see – the complete picture. At local council meetings he points out the consequences of any decision, the possibilities with every problem and new options when the alternatives seem lacking. Fredrick dampens wild extremes of behaviour. He is flexible and tries to do things in a logical order.

Fredrick loves new things and new people and his attachment to old friends and familiar places never stops him from moving on. He has an amazing capacity to 'get his head around' new situations and problems. He makes sense of chaos and creates a plan when there is none.

Rochelle Ringbond (cingulate gyrus) is closest to him and has a capacity for focus that matches his capacity to grasp the significance of a situation. However, Fredrick still maintains close friendships with two older women, Annie Almond (amygdala) and Priscilla Prizeman (nucleus accumbens). Although these two live in Midtown Cephalton and seem very different people he is in constant touch and takes careful note of Annie's concerns.

But it is Priscilla who has a special influence on him. He is so intellectual, ordered and measured but it is all boredom without the energy and drive that Priscilla evokes within him. He can look at Corrie O'Graphie and admire her sheer elegance and grace of movement. He can share all the business of everyday life with his true companion, Rochelle. He can, from time to time, even be completely captivated by the ageing, but still stunning, Annie Almond. But no-one can motivate him like Priscilla. Somehow she is the key to what makes Fredrick tick. She doesn't tell him what to do but she helps him to understand what is really important to him and Cephalton as a whole, what will make a difference, and she gives him the drive to do it, and to keep doing it, until he has what he wants.

The residents of Cephalton know that, despite Fredrick's apparent lack of emotion and slowness to respond, his priority is to match the demands and needs of the community with what can be done given the realities of the resources available. His leadership is highly respected even if at times he seems to be a damper on those who want action.

Although Fredrick usually keeps good health, when he is unwell it can have a profound effect on the whole of Cephalton. He becomes passive, indecisive and poverty-stricken for ideas. As a result the community is leaderless, lacking in the initiative, decisiveness and imagination that he usually provides. He can be silly, socially inappropriate and even very thoughtless and uncaring towards others. At the extreme of his illness, he is chaotic, impulsive, distractible and excitable with no real sense of direction in what he is doing. Most of the community seem helpless in response but some, such as Annie Almond and Priscilla Prizeman, take over and push through their own more limited agendas.

The frontal lobes explained

Location and structure

The frontal lobes constitute about one-third of the cortex and lie behind the forehead, above the eyes, and beneath the front half of the skull (see Figure 2.1). They are separated from the back of the brain by a ravine – the central sulcus – and from the temporal lobes by another ravine – the lateral or Sylvian fissure. The most posterior part of the frontal lobes is known as the primary motor cortex (this is covered in Chapter 4 Dudley Doit). Immediately in front of the primary motor cortex is the area known as the premotor (or secondary motor) cortex and Broca's area for language expression (see below and Chapter 5). The remaining half of the frontal lobes is known as the prefrontal cortex.

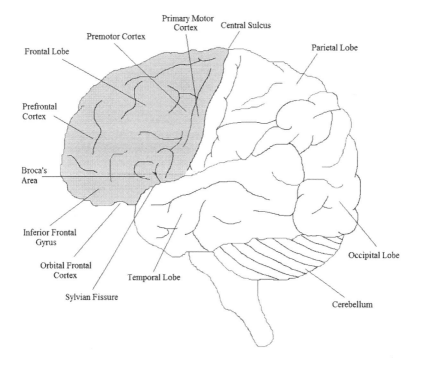

Figure 2.1. Lateral view (outer surface) of the left side of the brain showing the frontal lobes shaded in grey. Each main lobe of the brain which is visible is labelled.

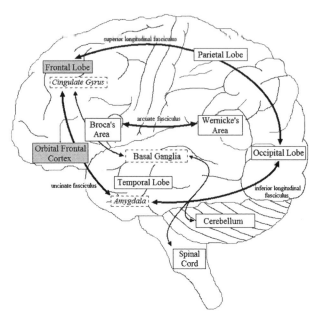

Figure 2.2. Lateral view (outer surface) of the left side of the brain showing a schematic representation of the main connections of the frontal lobes with other key areas of the brain.

Connections

The frontal lobes on either side of the brain are connected to each other by a bundle of fibres – the anterior commissure. The lower part of the frontal lobes – the orbitofrontal lobes – is connected to the front tip of the temporal lobes by another bundle of fibres, the uncinate fasciculus. This is a particularly important connection as it provides direct communication between the amygdala (Annie Almond, Chapter 13) – a vital centre for emotion processing – and the frontal lobes.

There are also two superhighways, huge long bundles of fibres, connecting the frontal lobes with the back of the brain: the superior longitudinal fasciculus and the inferior longitudinal fasciculus. They could almost be considered as the high road and the low road.

The superior longitudinal fasciculus reaches from the top of the front of the brain to the top of the back of the brain. As it passes around the centre of the brain it splits in two. One section, the arcuate fasciculus, sweeps down to link the centre for expressing speech in the front of the brain (Broca's area) to the centre for receiving speech towards the middle of the brain (Wernicke's area). We will meet these again in Chapter 5 (Cherry and Charles Chatterley). The other section of the superior longitudinal fasciculus travels to that part of the brain controlling vision – the occipital lobes (Penelope Panorama, Chapter 8). This superhighway keeps information flowing in relation to communication, ensuring that the command centres of the brain are well informed at all times.

The second superhighway, the inferior longitudinal fasciculus, linking the front to the back of the brain, takes the low road. It connects the lower parts of the frontal lobes to the lower parts of the temporal lobes, and connects the emotional systems of the brain with the command centres of the brain and with the information system coming from the outside world. It might be considered as the emotional super-highway. It has entries and exits all along the way, and is also connected to a ring road, the cingulate gyrus (Rochelle Ringbond, Chapter 3).

Another most important connection is between the frontal lobes and the spinal cord, allowing the production of movement. On the way this connection is joined by fibres from knots of tissue that lie deep in the brain called the basal ganglia (Corrie O'Graphie, Chapter 15). These regulate muscle tone and organise our movements into patterns or groups of coordinated movements. More fibres join these pathways from the cerebellum (Frank Finesse, Chapter 19) which keeps movement smooth and graceful.

Functions

The frontal lobes are the headquarters for running the rest of the brain, i.e. the executive centre. The key function is goal-oriented behaviour. Although the work of the frontal lobes and the associated systems have been given very abstract sounding titles such as executive functions, supervisory attentional systems and temporal schema regulation, in fact much of the work of the frontal lobes can be conceptualised quite simply as reconciling internal emotional states with the demands of external reality.

The main functions of the frontal lobes are to make sense of what is happening both internally and externally and how to address both simultaneously. They are crucial to making judgements, motivation, planning, making decisions and controlling behaviour. They are central to the formation of personality.

More subtly the frontal lobes enable flexible thinking, sequencing of actions, paying attention (including to more than one task at a time), detecting change (novelty detection), and utilising memory. These functions are reflected in the ability to change our mind when necessary, for example squeeze the tooth paste *after* picking up the tooth brush, keeping focused on the job at hand, noticing when something out of the ordinary happens, doing two jobs at once, and absorbing new information, e.g. remembering a telephone number until it can be written down. The executive functions of the frontal lobes are summarised below:

- Foresight and anticipation
- Focusing and sustaining attention
- Planning organising and prioritising
- Decision-making
- Reflecting
- Enthusiasm, motivation and persistence

The frontal lobes also play an important part in motor activity. The motor cortex, in the posterior section of the frontal lobes, is discussed in detail in Chapter 4 (Dudley Doit). The prefrontal cortex is also relevant to motor activity in that it constitutes a large network that connects the brain's motor, perceptual and limbic regions. These connections allow coordination of processing across wide regions of the central nervous system (CNS).

In summary, the frontal lobes are intensively involved in a wide range of activities, including thinking, perception, feeling, interpretation, planning, movement and speech – a very busy part of the brain.

When things go wrong

Dysfunction affecting structures as complex as the frontal lobe is associated with multiple, complex and far-reaching difficulties. Reduction in frontal lobe activity can lead to developmental delay, disinhibition and impulsivity, overeating and behavioural problems.

Children may be born with disorders that have a profound effect upon the frontal lobes. *Phenylketonuria* is an inborn error of metabolism in which the enzyme necessary to break down the amino acid phenylalanine is absent. In consequence there is a failure to convert phenylalanine to dopamine, an essential chemical for frontal lobe function. Even when placed on low phenylalanine diets these children may show difficulties in thinking and have lower IQs due to the restricted dopamine, particularly in the prefrontal cortex.

A common problem affecting the frontal lobes is *attention deficit hyperactivity disorder* (ADHD).

> Brendan, aged eight, was diagnosed with ADHD on the basis of severe behavioural and attentional difficulties. He was distractible, noisy, disruptive, and sometimes aggressive towards peers and teachers. He had been expelled from his previous school. His behaviour at home was not quite so bad, although he was overactive and impulsive. His mother had become exhausted from trying to control him at home and liaise with the school. Stimulant medication, combined with the provision of a low stimulus environment, continuous, firm and consistent limit-setting and the planning of his activities, led to considerable improvement.

Neuroimaging studies have shown that ADHD is consistently associated with alterations in structure and function in the frontal lobes as well as the basal ganglia and the cerebellum. Specifically there is decreased activity in the frontal lobes, which appears to be partly reversed with stimulant medication. The underactivity of the frontal lobes contributes to the restlessness, distractibility, impulsivity and aggression. In Brendan's case the stimulant medication clearly helped alleviate some of these phenomena. The stimulant medication triggers frontal activity. Meanwhile the provision by his mother of a low stimulus environment with the limit-setting and the planning of his activities functions as an 'external frontal lobe prosthesis'.

Head injuries involving the frontal lobes result in a very consistent pattern of problems. Patients often have difficulty with many different aspects of thinking as well as profound personality changes. The clinical presentation, where the frontal lobes take most of the impact, may look like schizophrenia, with confusion, delusions and hallucinations and subsequently a profound loss of motivation or a major personality problem.

> Tracey, 17, was referred following her attack on a 'bouncer' at a nightclub. She was 39 weeks pregnant. At five years of age she had been involved in a car accident in which both parents were killed and she had sustained an open head injury involving severe damage to both frontal lobes. She had been a developmentally normal, high-functioning child in a warm and supportive family prior to the accident.
>
> There were no extended family members and she was raised as a ward of the state. From as early as seven years of age it was clear she was showing features of conduct disorder, social disinhibition and attention deficit difficulties.
>
> Throughout her teens she was sexually promiscuous and oblivious to any social norms. She was aggressive to anyone who frustrated her and was afraid of no-one. Her child was removed at delivery because of fears for the child's safety and she showed no concern, distress, irritation or evidence of attachment.

Tracey's frontal lobe damage was responsible for changing her personality from a warm and caring girl to an antisocial, aggressive and disinhibited person. Antisocial behaviour, regardless of whether or not it is subsequent to brain injury, is associated with reduced frontal lobe activity.

Damage to the frontal lobes can occur from causes other than head injury.

> Catherine was a normal, healthy 15-year-old when she was trapped in a fire in the supermarket where she did part-time work. She suffered extensive full thickness burns to her legs and severe toxic fume

inhalation. Following recovery from her burns her family and friends noticed that she seemed strangely unconcerned about her injuries. Her friends at school no longer felt close to her and found her superficial and unempathic, although she was indiscriminately friendly. She could no longer plan her day and had great difficulty concentrating.

Catherine could not organise an essay – something she had been previously very good at doing. Her difficulties concentrating responded to methylphenidate but she remained prone to being indiscriminately friendly and to a superficial 'cocktail chatter' type of conversation. Psychological assessment revealed a marked deficit in the executive functions of planning, sequencing, problem-solving and social judgement.

Inhalation of toxic fumes such as carbon monoxide can have disastrous effects on the frontal lobes. Usually there is a persisting decrease in both blood flow and glucose metabolism. Such damage can also alter and impair a person's personality, responsiveness and ability to perform cognitive tasks that the person once found easy.

The classic frontal lobe case: Phineas Gage

Phineas Gage is perhaps the most famous case of a person with profound frontal lobe damage. Phineas was a railroad worker in Cavendish, USA in 1848. Prior to his head injury he was an exemplary citizen who worked hard and was energetic and was described as a clear thinker. He paid particular attention to managing his financial and personal affairs.

In 1848, at age 25, he was working on the railroad when he forgot to cover explosive powder with sand before he thrust down his tamping iron and the iron set off a spark that caused a large explosion. This explosion resulted in Phineas' tamping iron being forced upwards through his left check and out of the top of his head. It careered through the tissue and bone of Phineas' brain and skull and landed on the ground near him. Phineas remained conscious and was able to speak straight after the accident. He had his wounds cleaned and disinfected by a local doctor and was able to return home after two months.

It became apparent that after Phineas' medical injuries healed his intelligence and perceptual and motor abilities were still well intact. However, Phineas' personality had completely changed. He became impatient, rude and had regular angry outbursts. He was no longer able to follow a coherent plan and often rejected well-informed advice. He became so unreliable and unpredictable that he was sacked from his railroad job.

Phineas died at age 38 following violent epileptic seizures that resurfaced as remnants of his previous neurological trauma. Eventually Phineas' skull was placed in Harvard Medical School. Damasio and colleagues (1994) used brain imaging techniques to reconstruct Phineas' skull. It was found that the iron had destroyed the ventromedial aspects (the inner, under aspects of the frontal lobes towards the middle of the two hemispheres) of the most anterior portions of the frontal cortex in the right and left hemispheres. However, the motor and premotor cortices were not affected and hence Phineas had no problems with movement after the accident. The damaged part of his frontal lobes shows how important the frontal lobes are in evaluating significance of events and in regulating emotional responses (Gazzaniga, Ivry and Mangun 2007).

Fredrick Foresight in summary

Fredrick, mayor of Cephalton, lives with Rochelle Ringbond (cingulate gyrus) on a large estate in Uptown. He is the big-picture person who carefully considers all aspects of a problem, makes the decisions, provides motivation and gives the go-ahead. He, more than anyone, stamps his personality on the town. He is close to Priscilla Prizeman (nucleus accumbens) and Annie Almond (amygdala) and is also sensitive to the responses of Rosie Reaction (autonomic nervous system). When he is unwell the whole town is affected with multiple, complex and far-reaching consequences.

References

Damasio, H., Grabowski, T., Frank, R., Galaburda, A.M. and Damasio, A.R. (1994) 'The return of Phineas Gage: Clues about the brain from the skull of a famous patient.' *Science* *264*, 1102–1105.

Gazzaniga, M.S., Ivry, R.B. and Mangun, G.R. (2007) *Cognitive Neuroscience: The Biology of the Mind.* New York, NY: Norton.

Further reading

Salloway, S., Mallory, P. and Duffy, J. (2001) *The Frontal Lobes and Neuropsychiatric Illness.* Washington DC and London: American Psychiatric Publishers.

Chapter 3

Rochelle Ringbond: the Cingulate Gyrus

Meet Rochelle Ringbond

Rochelle lives in Uptown Cephalton with her partner, the town mayor, Fredrick Foresight (frontal lobe) but less obviously spends much of her time with Maurice Mapply (parietal lobe). She exemplifies the successful, modern woman. She is sensitive, highly focused and networks well and widely. She loves children and is sensitive to the pain of others and to environmental issues. Her ability to focus includes her extraordinary skill at detecting errors and sources of conflict. Her networking skills enable her to organise and drive others and she regularly engages in fact-finding tours for business and cultural exchanges with other communities.

As Fredrick's partner she offers a counterbalance to his cool objectivity and she keeps others from taking up his time with insignificant detail. Rochelle is also closely connected with Priscilla Prizeman (nucleus accumbens), Annie Almond (amygdala) and Sage Seahorse (hippocampus). But the only person who can unsettle Rochelle's legendary ability to focus is Maurice Mapply who, more than anyone, can capture her attention and shift her focus.

There can be a dark side to Rochelle. When she is unwell it is hard to recognise her as the same person. She can become miserable, depressed, and less empathic toward others. Rochelle is then thoughtless and rigid in her thinking. She starts to fuss over minor details, checks repeatedly lest she has done anything wrong and cannot let go of an issue, especially the negative aspects of her past. At such times, Rochelle becomes argumentative, uncooperative and fights with others. At worst she becomes profoundly apathetic and stops talking, walking and communicating. The impact on the town would be calamitous if she did not return to her normal self.

The cingulate gyrus explained

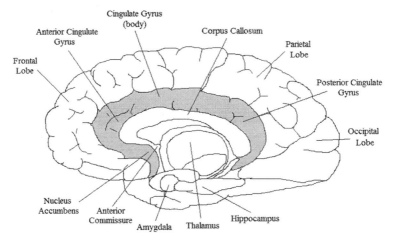

Figure 3.1. Medial view (inner surface) of the right side of the brain showing the cingulate gyrus shaded in grey. Each of the main visible lobes of the brain is labelled.

Location and structure

The crescent-shaped cingulate gyrus is broadly divided into two main parts, stretching from the front to the back of the brain, the anterior cingulate (part of the frontal lobe) and the posterior cingulate (part of the parietal lobe). It sits over and on either side of the great bridge (corpus callosum – Christopher Crosstalk, see Chapter 11) between the two halves of the brain.

Connections

The cingulate gyrus' connections are best considered by distinguishing between the anterior and posterior cingulate gyrus. The anterior

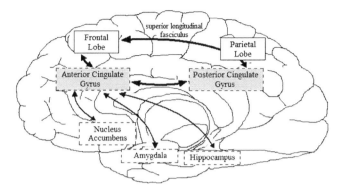

Figure 3.2. Medial view (inner surface) of the right side of the brain showing a schematic representation of the main connections between the cingulate gyrus and other key areas of the brain.

cingulate gyrus is the meeting place between the thinking brain (frontal lobes) and the feeling brain (limbic system). It has strong connections with the rest of the frontal lobes and with limbic structures such as the nucleus accumbens, amygdala and hippocampus. The posterior cingulate gyrus is the meeting place between the thinking brain and the perceptual brain (parietal lobes) and has strong connections with the frontal lobes and the superior parietal lobes.

Taken as a whole the cingulate gyrus might be likened to a ring road, not taking the most direct route, but having a considerable number of connections on the way.

Functions

The location and connections ensure that the cingulate gyrus has multiple functions, too various and complex to detail in depth but the key functions are listed below:

- Attention

- Goal-directed behaviour

- Emotional processing (empathy and attachment)

ATTENTION

The cingulate plays a critical role in coordinating activity across attention systems. This activity is sometimes known as the 'supervisory attention system' or 'executive attention system'. It aids attention by filtering out irrelevant stimuli (selective attention) and by amplifying activity in one perceptual mode over another (sustained attention). This is particularly important in situations where attention is divided. Position emission tomography (PET) scan studies show the anterior cingulate gyrus to be active during tasks which involve scrutinising stimuli and selecting responses. It seems to be particularly relevant to situations of conflict and difficulty in knowing what to do. This is vividly illustrated during the Stroop task (see Technical corner later in the chapter). The more novel and difficult is the situation to interpret, then the more likely it is that the cingulate gyrus is involved.

GOAL-DIRECTED BEHAVIOUR

Another key function of the cingulate is that of goal-directed behaviour. This is dependent upon the executive functions discussed in Chapter 2 (thinking, planning, decision-making and initiating action). The cingulate provides a filtering mechanism to prioritise the relevant factors in the decision-making process.

EMOTIONAL PROCESSING, EMPATHY AND ATTACHMENT

The third key function of the cingulate is that of emotional processing which occurs through its strong connections both to the frontal lobes and to the limbic system. The cingulate is central to enabling the connection of thoughts and feelings (to think about feelings and to feel in response to thoughts). This ability to connect thoughts and feelings is integral to empathy, affection and attachment.

When things go wrong

A number of conditions arise associated with cingulate dysfunction.

DEPRESSION

Brain imaging studies have confirmed the role of the anterior cingulate in depression. The main attentional systems are impaired with much reduced concentration. The loss of the ability to know what is and is not important results in indecisiveness. Loss of goal-directed behaviour is demonstrated by social withdrawal and loss of interest. Abnormal emotional processing includes the inability to experience pleasure, empathy and normal attachment. In extreme depression, resistant to all treatments, deep brain stimulation of the anterior cingulate has been shown to be effective in small sample, uncontrolled studies.

OBSESSIVE COMPULSIVE DISORDER (OCD)

In OCD brain imaging has shown increased blood flow in the cingulate gyrus. This seems to be associated with an inability to shift attention from the intrusive and distressing thoughts (cognitive inflexibility), and therefore a compulsion to take what would be usually considered inappropriate actions to reduce the distress. Goal-directed behaviour is impaired with consequent compulsive behaviour such as repetitive checking. Abnormal emotional processing is demonstrated by excessive fear and doubt. In the most severe forms of OCD surgical incision of the cingulate (leading to disconnection between the basal ganglia and the frontal lobes) has been shown to reduce obsessions and compulsions.

> Emma, 14, had always been slightly perfectionist, wanting everything to be clean and tidy all the time. More recently she had insisted that her mother repeatedly washed all the pans, cutlery and crockery to ensure their cleanliness. Emma cleaned and dusted her bedroom several times a day and refused to use the bathroom until the toilet, bath and sink had been scrubbed with disinfectant. She was tearful much of the time and angry when her requests were challenged or resisted, insisting that the whole family was at risk of infection and disease. Her school work suffered through her inability to concentrate.

Similar features are found in anorexia nervosa with an inability to shift attention from the intrusive and distressing thoughts of being fat and greedy, and therefore a compulsion to avoid food and lose weight.

AKINETIC MUTISM

This rare condition is manifested by complete loss of speech and movement whilst still appearing to be alert. This is believed to be due to extreme cingulate dysfunction.

> Mustafa, aged 12, who had received chemotherapy and radiotherapy for a brain tumour, stopped talking and became totally immobile while still appearing fully conscious. Magnetic resonance imaging (MRI) scan suggested severe inflammatory scarring in the cingulate region. As he began to improve with intensive psychopharmacological and occupational therapy he became depressed and showed signs of obsessive compulsive disorder, suggesting improvement in cingulate function. Ultimately he made a full recovery.

Technical corner

The Stroop task (Macleod, 1991) involves a subject being presented with a list of words that spell out the names of the colours that are either matching or non-matching to the ink colour. In both conditions, the subject is asked to name the colour of the words, inhibiting the natural tendency to read the words themselves (Gazzaniga, Ivry and Mangun 2007).

The Stroop task	
Colour matches word	Colour does not match word
RED	GREEN
GREEN	BLUE
RED	RED
BLUE	BLUE
BLUE	GREEN
GREEN	RED
BLUE	GREEN

When the colour and the word match, there is no conflict. However, when there is a mismatch between the colour and the word, there is conflict for the participant, who must overcome the temptation to read the words and instead focus on the ink colour. The anterior cingulate is at its most active when there is a mismatch between the colour and the word.

Rochelle Ringbond in summary

Rochelle Ringbond plays a critical part in the life of Cephalton, being one of its great networkers. She is intimately involved with Fredrick but also has a close relationship with Maurice and has many friendships in Midtown. Through all her connections she and Fredrick are able to focus on what the town really needs and wants. Her care, empathy and nurture of others are complementary to Fredrick's intellectual objectivity. When unwell she can become slow and indecisive with consequent effect on the whole community.

References

Gazzaniga, M.S., Ivry, R.B. and Mangun, G.R. (2007) *Cognitive Neuroscience: The Biology of the Mind.* New York, NY: Norton.

MacLeod, C. (1991) 'Half a century of research on the Stroop effect: An integrative review.' *Psychological Bulletin 109,* 163–120.

Further reading

Brizendine, L. (2006) *The Female Brain.* New York, NY: Broadway Books.

Bush, G., Luu, P. and Posner, M.I. (2000) 'Cognitive and emotional influences in anterior cingulate cortex.' *Trends in Cognitive Science 4,* 215–222.

Rosenberg, D. and Keshaven, M. (1998) 'Toward a neurodevelopmental model of obsessive compulsive disorder.' *Biological Psychiatry 43,* 623–640.

Chapter 4

Dudley Doit: the Motor Cortex

Meet Dudley Doit

Dudley Doit lives on the Foresight Estate with his love, Cherry Chatterley (Broca's area). They live along the northern side of the Great Canyon (central sulcus) which divides the North and the South of Uptown Cephalton. Dudley and Cherry work well together, with her doing the talking and him getting on with the job. A real action man and very much in command of his body, he works out in the Cephalton gym, where he has a close working partnership with Melissa Mirrorwood (somatosensory cortex). But his influence stretches far beyond the gym – he seems to be involved with all the town's activities.

Dudley looks up to Fredrick Foresight (frontal lobes) and follows his lead in almost all he does. He also tries to coordinate his activities with those of Melissa at every step. He works out with Frank Finesse (cerebellum) and Corrie O'Graphie (basal ganglia) who are always willing to help him with his exercise routines. Dudley also relates well to Fay Faceandear (pons) who can always bring a smile to his face with her wonderful capacity to act.

But even the very muscular Dudley can become unwell. Sometimes when he is tired everything he does seems to become more chaotic and disorganised. He has had times in his life when he has become clumsy and unable to do ordinary day-to-day things, such as tying his shoe laces or standing on one foot to put on his trousers. At other times of ill health he has difficulty moving.

The motor cortex explained

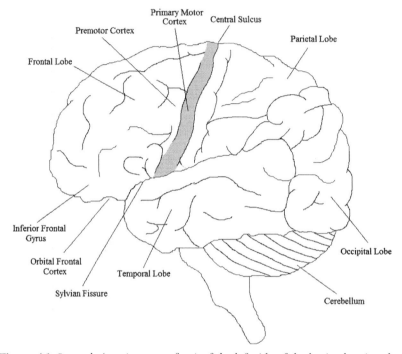

Figure 4.1. Lateral view (outer surface) of the left side of the brain showing the primary motor cortex shaded in grey. Each of the main visible lobes of the brain is labelled.

Location and structure

The motor cortex forms part of the frontal lobes and is located immediately in front of the large divide between the front and back halves of the brain (central sulcus). It consists of two main parts: the premotor cortex anteriorly and the primary motor cortex posteriorly.

Connections

The motor cortex has connections with the remainder of the frontal lobes, including Broca's area, and with the somatosensory cortex, the basal ganglia, the cerebellum, the brain stem and the spinal cord.

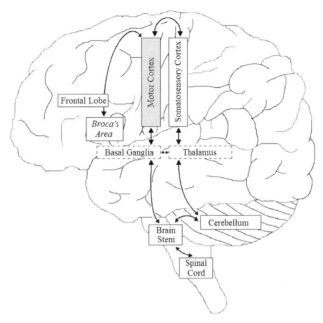

Figure 4.2. Lateral view (outer surface) of the left side of the brain showing a schematic representation of the main connections of the motor cortex with other key areas of the brain.

Functions

The motor cortex is involved exclusively in movement and its various components. Functions of the motor cortex are:

- The planning of movement
- The initiation of movement
- The monitoring and maintaining of movement

THE PLANNING OF MOVEMENT

This occurs as a result of collaboration between the frontal, the somatosensory and the premotor cortex (anterior motor cortex). The frontal lobes provides goal-directed behaviour, the somatosensory cortex provides information with regard to where the body is in space, and the premotor cortex coordinates this information and then instructs the primary motor cortex (posterior motor cortex).

THE INITIATION OF MOVEMENT

This occurs as a result of the instructions sent by the premotor to the primary motor cortex. This in turn sends messages both to the brain stem and onward to the nerves that supply the voluntary muscles of the head and neck and particularly the face. The motor aspects of speech specifically are initiated by Broca's area, found immediately next to the primary motor cortex (see Chapter 5). Messages are also sent from the primary motor cortex to the spinal cord to supply the voluntary muscles of the rest of the body. The basal ganglia and cerebellum add sophistication to movement with the basal ganglia focusing on detail and the cerebellum on timing.

THE MONITORING AND MAINTAINING OF MOVEMENT

This occurs as a result of sensory feedback which is monitored by the frontal lobes and a subsequent repetition of the above cycle.

When things go wrong

There are three types of problem that can affect the motor cortex, corresponding with each of its three functions.

PROBLEMS WITH PLANNING MOVEMENT

A breakdown in the communication between the premotor, somatosensory and frontal lobes (sensory–motor integration) leads to an inability to plan movement, and therefore correctly initiate it (dyspraxia).

> Every day at breakfast John, aged six, would spill his milk as he tried to drink it. His teacher was worried by how often he fell compared with other children. His mother had noticed that he squeezed the tooth paste before the brush was ready. His older brother had none of these problems at the same age.

Developmental dyspraxia, like that of John, is more common in boys and is due to a delay in sensory–motor integration. Other causes of dyspraxia include cerebrovascular accidents and trauma within the premotor cortex.

PROBLEMS WITH INITIATING MOVEMENT

Such problems arise due to a breakdown in communication between the primary motor cortex and the voluntary muscles. If such breakdown occurs within the brain or spinal cord it is known as an upper motor neurone lesion; if it occurs outside the brain or spinal cord it is known as a lower motor neurone lesion. Both of these problems result in an inability to initiate movement, i.e. paralysis. Upper motor neurone paralysis leads to spasticity (increased muscle tone) and lower motor neurone paralysis leads to flaccidity (decreased muscle tone).

PROBLEMS WITH MONITORING AND MAINTAINING MOVEMENT

These arise from failure of sensory feedback from the somatosensory to the frontal lobes and back into the planning and initiating cycle described above.

> Cheryl, aged eight, had suffered perinatal hypoxia with major delay in developmental milestones. Her movements had a staccato quality and her speech was slurred. She had a squint which was worse when she was tired and she frequently bumped into furniture. She was diagnosed with cerebral palsy as characterised by her lack of sensory–motor integration.

The perinatal hypoxia damaged the essential pathways for providing the feedback for maintaining and monitoring movement.

Technical corner

The motor cortex has a complex system of ensuring that its messages arrive at the intended destination. For example, if we wish to raise a glass the message from the motor cortex must reach the hand. The ingenious method for doing this involves every voluntary muscle in the body having a designated part of the motor cortex. This 'muscle map' is known as the 'motor homunculus' (little human) – see Figure 4.3.

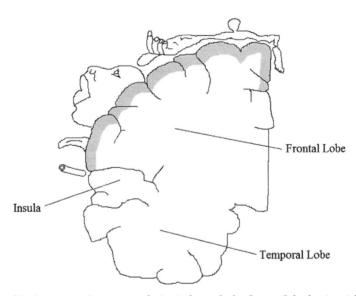

Figure 4.3. A cross section (coronal view) through the front of the brain with a pictorial representation of those parts of the body that are controlled by the primary motor cortex. Each of the visible lobes are labelled.

Dudley Doit in summary

Dudley, partner to Cherry Chatterley, is a man of action and a team player, with a huge impact on all around him, whether in the town or the shire. His mentor is Fredrick Foresight but he tries to keep in step with

Melissa Mirrorwood when they work out in the gym. Corrie O'Graphie and Frank Finesse have a strong influence on his repertoire and sophistication of exercise routines. When he is unwell he can become clumsy or paralysed.

Further reading

Gazzaniga, M.S., Ivry, R.B. and Mangun, G.R. (2007) *Cognitive Neuroscience: The Biology of Mind.* New York, NY: Norton.

Kalat, J. (2007) *Biological Psychology.* Belmont, CA: Wadsworth Language Learning.

Chapter 5

Cherry and Charles Chatterley: Broca's and Wernicke's Areas

Meet Cherry and Charles Chatterley

Cherry (Broca's area) and Charles Chatterley (Wernicke's area) are twins. They both live in Uptown Cephalton, Cherry with Dudley Doit (motor cortex) on the estate owned by Fredrick Foresight (frontal lobes) and Charles at the other side of the Great Canyon (central sulcus), which divides the North and the South of Uptown Cephalton.

Although Cherry's closest friend is her brother, Charles, she is also on very good terms with Brenda Bridgehead (insula), Corrie O'Graphie (basal ganglia), Frank Finesse (cerebellum) and Annie Almond (amygdala).

Charles' friends include Melissa Mirrorwood (somatosensory cortex), Maurice Mapply (parietal lobe), Lilly Listentale (temporal lobe), Sage Seahorse (hippocampus), Annie Almond (amygdala), and Felicity Feelall (thalamus). But there are very few people with whom Charles shares what he really thinks and feels. This he reserves for Cherry and for Brenda Bridgehead, who is the only person with whom both Cherry and Charles share their deepest feelings, and she with them.

Cherry is the lead TV and radio personality in Cephalton, reading the News each day and reporting on any major event. She is said to be like the French side of the family, highly expressive, articulate, creative and making a point of being grammatically correct in everything she says while still maintaining panache and professionalism. Although she is the public voice of what is happening she has a whole team of people who help her to present the News, many of whom live nearby in Uptown Cephalton. Her life-long love, Dudley Doit, helps in every way he can but he appreciates that she is a virtuoso.

Charles is quite different from his twin sister. He is an attentive listener, which helps in his job as a telephonist in the Cephalton central community telephone exchange. Here he coordinates teleconferences both between residents of Cephalton and with the world outside. He is quiet and studious and uses his spare time to develop his passion – lexicography. His dictionary of favourite words, which he has compiled and archived over the years, contains about 50,000 words – words that mean more to him rather than just a random collection. He has a special interest in nouns.

Together they make a great team. Cherry is skilful at speaking and Charles at listening. Cherry impresses everyone in Cephalton with her extraordinary capacity to express herself. Charles, on the other hand, is often over-looked until it is clear that everyone is getting confused and needs someone who can make sense of the most difficult situations and of a myriad of conflicting messages. He coordinates and then lets Cherry know the true situation so that she, in turn, can let everyone know what is going on clearly and precisely.

When Charles or Cherry are unwell it soon becomes obvious that something is wrong. Cherry loses her eloquent and flowing speech. Everything becomes an effort, even expressing the most basic ideas. She starts talking in short, telegraphic-like sentences with the biggest problems being the shortest words such as 'if', 'and', 'or', 'but'. Her normal pedantic use of grammar is lost and if others use sentences that require correct grammar to understand them, she misses the point. On one occasion she was told by her team that a man had been killed by his wife and she announced on the evening News that *the man* had killed his wife. It is distressing to watch her speaking as if she is in pain and can only manage to communicate the most basic ideas in short explosive bursts. She understands most of what is said to her and can often indicate by gestures and pantomime-type actions what she wants to say. She cannot repeat what others have said to her but does seem to have clear thinking in the way she acts and communicates. In these circumstances she becomes understandably frustrated and then depressed.

When Charles is unwell it has an even bigger impact on Cephalton, despite his lower profile. First, it has a powerful effect on Cherry who becomes quite muddled in what she does, and the News doesn't quite make as much sense as usual. When Charles loses his greatest strength – the ability to listen and make sense of what others inside and outside the town are saying – the whole community feels isolated, from each other and from the outside world. At times it appears as if he is really unwell, with jumbled thoughts and speech, and seeming angry and paranoid. It is actually his ability to choose the right word that is affected rather than his thoughts. Finding the names of people, animals or objects becomes difficult. Whilst he can still talk at full speed the words come out wrongly with slight errors of meaning or sound. Sometimes he cannot repeat even simple phrases or understand what others are telling him. Hardest of all for him he cannot find many of the nouns that he has collected over the years and that he loves so much.

Perhaps the worst situation is when Cherry and Charles have both been ill at the same time. There is no News broadcast and the telephone system does not work. Communication has broken down.

Broca's and Wernicke's areas explained

Location and structure

Broca's area (Cherry), named after the famous French physician and anthropologist Pierre Paul Broca (1824–1880), is located in the left frontal lobe (Fredrick Foresight), close to the motor cortex (Dudley Doit). It looks a little like a heart and it is the 'heart' of the system for expressing thoughts. Wernicke's area (Charles Chatterley),

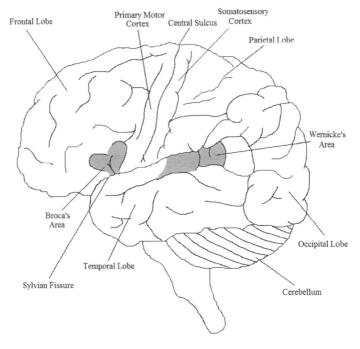

Figure 5.1. Lateral view (outer surface) of the left side of the brain, showing Broca's and Wernicke's areas shaded in grey. Each of the main visible lobes of the brain is labelled.

a banana-shaped structure, named after the Polish psychiatrist and neuropathologist, Karl Wernicke (1848–1905), is in the posterior, superior (uppermost) part of the temporal lobe and adjacent to the parietal lobe (Maurice Mapply).

Broca's area and Wernicke's area are located predominantly on the left side of the brain. Over 97 per cent of right handers and 60 per cent of left handers speak with the left side of their brain. The remainder of the left handers tend to use both sides of the brain for language.

Connections

Broca's area and Wernicke's area are connected to each other by a bundle of nerve fibres known as 'the arcuate fasciculus' which connects them via the insula (Brenda Bridgehead). Broca's area is connected to those parts

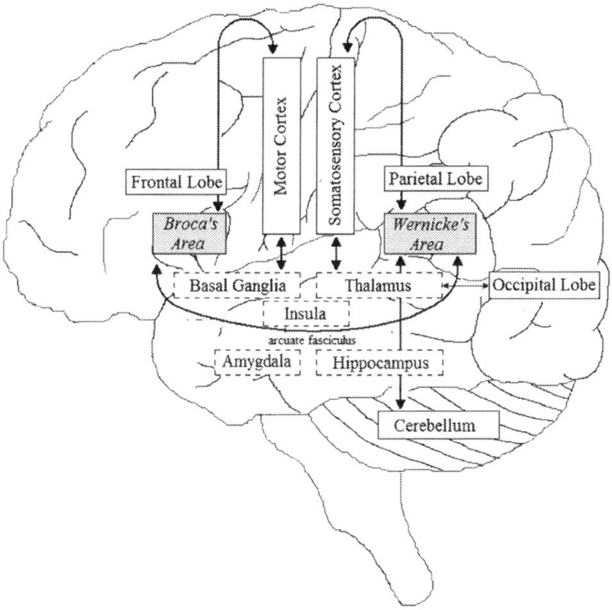

Figure 5.2. Lateral view (outer surface) of the left side of the brain showing a schematic representation of the main connections of Broca's and Wernicke's areas with other key areas of the brain. Note the critical role of the arcuate fasciculus and insula in connecting expressive and receptive areas of speech.

of the brain associated with movement, including the motor cortex (Dudley Doit), the basal ganglia (Corrie O'Graphie) and the cerebellum (Frank Finesse). It is also connected to the emotional centres including the amygdala (Annie Almond). Wernicke's area is connected to those parts of the brain associated with sensation, including the somatosensory cortex (Melissa Mirrorwood), the parietal lobe (Maurice Mapply), the occipital lobe (Penelope Panorama) and the thalamus (Felicity Feelall). Wernicke's area is also connected to emotional centres such as the amygdala and the memory centres such as the hippocampus.

Functions

The key function of Broca's and Wernicke's areas is communication, Broca's focusing more on expression and Wernicke's on reception.

Together they enable all aspects of speech to be woven together into coherent communication.

Key functions of Broca's area	Key functions of Wernicke's area
* Expression	* Reception
* Converting ideas into words	* Converting words into ideas
* Initiating speech	* Analysing speech
* Flow of speech	* Content of speech
* Grammar	* Meaning

Broca's area converts ideas into words, and then expresses the words through the muscular movements of speech. It ensures the flow of speech and correct grammar, especially with words of action such as verbs. Wernicke's area converts the words of others into ideas, by analysing their content and meaning.

The arcuate fasciculus is the main connection between Broca's area and Wernicke's area. It enables constant communication between the two centres in order to combine their skills. Also, through its passage via the insula, it enables the emotional understanding and expression of language. However, there are also connections between Broca's and Wernicke's areas and other parts of the brain. Smoothness of articulation is enabled through connections with the basal ganglia and cerebellum. The integration of all the sensations involved in communication (e.g. vision, sound, touch) occurs through the somatosensory cortex. Memories of meaning are integrated through connections with the hippocampus.

When things go wrong

When problems occur affecting Broca's area, Wernicke's area or the connections between them, communication is jeopardised. The most significant of such problems are the dysphasias and autism.

THE DYSPHASIAS

These are broadly divided into 'expressive or Broca's dysphasia', 'receptive or Wernicke's dysphasia', 'conductive dysphasia', 'mixed dysphasia' and 'global dysphasia'. The extreme form of dysphasia is known as 'aphasia' when the ability to speak is lost. The most common causes of the dysphasias are cerebrovascular accidents (strokes), trauma, infection and tumours.

BROCA'S DYSPHASIA

Patients with this type of dysphasia usually have good understanding of speech but difficulty expressing what they want to say. Such people speak very slowly, with great effort and often some distress. Later they become resigned and depressed. Intriguingly deaf people who have damage in Broca's area have difficulty producing sign language although they can use their hands well in other ways.

> Paul, a Professor of English, was a fine scholar and lecturer and highly regarded by his colleagues and students. At the age of 61 he had a stroke due to a bleed from his middle cerebral artery (superior branch) affecting his brain in and around Broca's area. Consequently, his speech became short, and staccato with words such as 'the', 'it', 'their' and 'a' were omitted. For example, when describing to his wife that he had been at physiotherapy during the morning, he said 'Took…physio…morning… hurt'. Initially he was frustrated and angry at his inability to express himself. Subsequently he became depressed.

WERNICKE'S DYSPHASIA

Wernicke's dysphasia involves difficulty in understanding speech. The flow of speech is normal but its sense is lost. There is an inability to find the names of objects (anomia) and sometimes names for objects are fabricated (neologism), e.g. 'strapper' instead of 'belt'.

> Jill, aged 70, had been living in a nursing home for the past two years. She had suffered a stroke in her middle cerebral artery (inferior branch)

which supplies Wernicke's area and its surrounds. As she began to recover, she had continued difficulty with her ability to understand what other people were saying to her and she in turn was difficult to understand. She had always been a friendly person who loved to chat with others, but now found mixing with others difficult.

CONDUCTIVE, MIXED AND GLOBAL DYSPHASIAS

Sometimes Broca's and Wernicke's areas remain intact but the connection between them (arcuate fasciculus) is impaired. This leads to difficulties in linking receptive and expressive speech (conductive dysphasia). Most commonly, however, speech problems consist of combinations of these clinical pictures (mixed dysphasia). When all of these dysphasias are present the term global dysphasia is applied.

The classic Broca's area case: Monsieur Leborgne (Tan)

The most famous patient of the French surgeon Paul Broca was Monsieur Leborgne who remained in the Bicetre Hospital where Broca was working for many years. He had been paralysed down his right side for over 30 years from a neurosyphilitic lesion in the left side of his brain and was only able to speak the words 'tan, tan'. Hence, Leborgne was often called Tan. He died of septicaemia and gangrene of his right leg.

At the post-mortem, Broca discovered a lesion on the surface of the left side of the frontal lobe of Leborgne's brain. This discovery was one of the main events leading to Broca's discovery of the area now bearing his name and his discovering its function in speech production. Leborgne's brain can still be viewed in Paris at the Dupuytren Museum.

Cherry and Charles Chatterley in summary

The twins Cherry (Broca's area) and Charles (Wernicke's area) are at the centre of communication in Cephalton. Cherry's strength is in speaking and Charles' in listening. Cherry, who lives and works with Dudley Doit (motor cortex), and Charles have a close relationship. When either is unwell communication both within Cephalton and between Cephalton and the outside world is impaired.

Further reading

Berko Gleason, J. (1993) *The Development of Language*, 3rd edition. New York, NY: Macmillian.

Kalat, J. (2007) *Biological Psychology*, 8th edition. Belmont, CA: Wadsworth Language Learning.

Selnes, O.A. and Hillis, A. (2000) 'Patient Tan revisited: A case of atypical global aphasia?' *Journal of the History of the Neurosciences 9*, 233–237.

Chapter 6

Melissa Mirrorwood: the Somatosensory Cortex

Meet Melissa Mirrorwood

Melissa Mirrorwood lives in Midtown just south of the Great Dividing Ravine (central sulcus) which separates North Cephalton from South Cephalton. She lives with the much older, but still very aware and physically fit, Maurice Mapply (parietal lobes). Neighbours include Lilly Listentale (temporal lobes), Brenda Bridgehead (insula), and Felicity Feelall (thalamus). Across the great dividing ravine, on the Foresight Estate, is Dudley Doit (motor cortex), with whom she runs the Cephalton gym.

Melissa is an elite athlete who likes to keep her body 'trim, taut and terrific'. She is a very physical and tactile sort of person and deeply aware of her own body, her own appearance and the appearances of those around her. She is extremely sensitive to the vibes and positioning going on about her and to the pain and temperature of any situation. She has a fine touch for the most subtle of circumstances but also can take pressure when needed. When pampered and feeling good, Melissa has a way of drawing everyone's attention to what it means to live in such a beautiful town and region. She is one of those people who learns more by touch than by talk and more by appearance than reputation. When Melissa sizes people up, appearances *do* matter.

Melissa and her partner, Maurice, share an interest in the world outside Cephalton, although Melissa is more enthusiastic about the

Shire and Maurice the world beyond. A little-known secret is that Melissa has a huge tattoo of a map of the Shire of Cephalton, for which she has a pet name 'Ho-Munculus'.

She keeps in touch with the rest of the town and Shire through her gossiping with her neighbours, Felicity and Brenda, about all that is happening.

When Melissa is unwell she gradually comes to believe that she is fat and ugly, and then has a particular preoccupation with the size of her stomach, hips and thighs. Occasionally, the size or shape of other body parts distresses her, even to the point of her seeking cosmetic surgery, although others can see nothing wrong. At other times she has lost sensation in parts of her body.

The somatosensory cortex explained

Location and structure

The somatosensory cortex is found just behind the deep divide between the front and back of the brain, the central sulcus, and medial to the sylvian or lateral fissure. It lies above the thalamus and corpus callosum and is in fact a specialised part of the parietal lobe.

The somatosensory cortex is divided into two main parts: the primary and secondary. The primary forms the majority of the somatosensory cortex and corresponds to the integration of sensation. The secondary is a small area at the base and corresponds to the representation of body image.

Connections

The somatosensory cortex receives information via the thalamus (Felicity Feelall) from the rest of the body regarding pain, vibration, body position, sense, touch, pain and temperature. There are outputs from the somatosensory cortex to the motor cortex (Dudley Doit), as well as back to the thalamus (Felicity Feelall), the insula (Brenda Bridgehead) and the parietal lobes (Maurice Mapply).

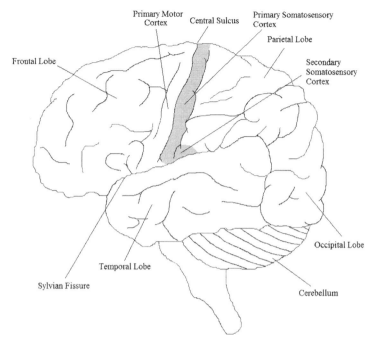

Figure 6.1. Lateral view (outer surface) of the left side of the brain showing the somatosensory cortex shaded in grey. Each of the main visible lobes of the brain is labelled.

Functions

The somatosensory cortex is mainly concerned with bodily sensation and body image:

- Processing body sensations
- Construction of body image
- Awareness of body position and state

BODILY SENSATION

The somatosensory cortex plays an important part in the processing of all the body sensations except for smell. These include the experience of pain, temperature, visceral state, light and deep touch, vibration, vision and hearing. It receives and integrates these sensations and then relays the information to other brain parts.

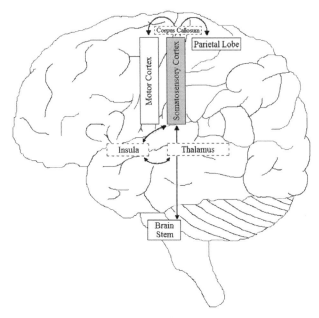

Figure 6.2. Lateral view (outer surface) of the brain showing a schematic representation of the main connections of the somatosensory cortex with other key areas of the brain. Note that it is the right somatosensory cortex that is dominant, unlike speech.

BODY IMAGE

The somatosensory cortex is critical for construction of body image. It provides a comprehensive and integrated map of current body state, including weight and shape, and then forwards this information primarily to the insula.

The body is represented in the somatosensory cortex in the form of a 'body map', known as the homunculus, Latin for 'little human' (Melissa's tattoo). Each part of the body is represented, not to a scale of its actual size but at a size equivalent to the amount of sensory representation. For example, the face, hands and genitals have the greatest representation and the trunk, limbs and internal organs the least.

When things go wrong

Dysfunction affecting the somatosensory cortex may lead to impairments of sensory processing and body image.

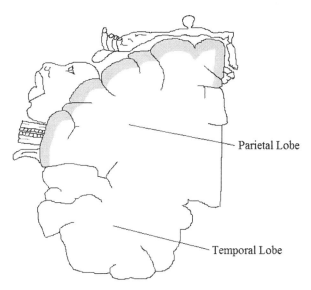

Figure 6.3. Coronal (cross section looking from the front) of the parietal lobes of the brain showing the parts of the somatosensory cortex that receive sensation from different parts of the body. It is referred to as the somatosensory homunculus (Latin for 'little human').

CEREBROVASCULAR ACCIDENTS/STROKES

Cerebrovascular accidents (CVAs or strokes) are the most common cause of dysfunction affecting the somatosensory cortex. In such circumstances there is an interruption of blood supply to the affected part of the brain.

> John, 56, had had high blood pressure for many years and had recently discontinued his medication. Whilst at work in his accounting firm he experienced difficulty concentrating, followed by a sensation of heat and tingling in his left hand. Later he noticed numbness throughout the left side of his body. When he stood up he stumbled. Examination revealed very high blood pressure and investigations showed a haemorrhage on the right side of his brain mainly affecting the (primary) somatosensory cortex.

Strokes commonly affect sensation because of the frequency with which the somatosensory cortex is involved. John's case illustrates the alterations in sense of touch, pain and temperature together with the effects of altered blood supply to other parts of the brain giving rise to impaired concentration and difficulties in movement.

ANOREXIA NERVOSA

Another condition involving the somatosensory cortex is anorexia nervosa, one of the key components of which is body image disturbance.

> Emma, 14, had been dieting for six months, having been teased at school about being overweight. Subsequently, although she had lost four kilos and was slightly below normal weight for her age and height, she expressed considerable distress at being 'too fat'. No amount of persuasion would convince her otherwise. She intensified her efforts to lose weight and would frequently make herself vomit. When questioned about how she saw herself she stated that although her face and arms were okay, she was absolutely convinced that her stomach, hips and thighs were enormous.

Emma illustrates the body image disturbance so characteristic of anorexia nervosa. Disconnection between the somatosensory cortex and other brain structures, especially the insula, leads to loss of accurate feedback about body shape and size to the rest of the brain.

PHANTOM LIMB

The somatosensory cortex is integrally involved in the sensations associated with phantom limb following amputation. When a body part – limb or other – has been amputated there is still a sensation as if the amputated part is still there. This experience can range from a slight tingling to intense pain.

> Carlos, 42, suffered the loss of his right arm in a motor bike accident when he was 35. He continues to have pain as if his elbow, wrist and fingers are still intact. The pain could be triggered by light touch to the right side of his face and to the right shoulder.

The part of the somatosensory cortex that had previously represented Carlos' right arm continued to be activated. However, the trigger for activation was now from those parts of the body that lie nearby the representations in the somatosensory cortex of the right arm, i.e. face and shoulder. Over time the representations in the somatosensory cortex of the lost arm diminish and the representations of the face and shoulders increase. Ramachandran and Blakeslee (1999) have drawn attention to this phenomenon in relation to the loss of a leg with increased representation of the genital region, leading to heightened genital sensitivity.

Technical corner

Experience can influence the somatosensory cortex. For example, if someone has played a string instrument for many years, the somatosensory cortex has an enlarged representation of the fingers of the left hand. It has also been shown that in Braille proofreaders the brain representation of the index finger is measurably larger at the end of a workday than at the same time on a vacation. Such changes may represent either collateral sprouting of axons or increased receptor sensitivity by the post-synaptic neurons. The cortex undergoes a slight reorganisation to enable extra representation of the information that a person uses the most.

Melissa Mirrorwood in summary

Melissa Mirrorwood (somatosensory cortex) lives immediately south of the Great Divide with her partner, Maurice Mapply (parietal lobe). She is extremely sensitive to the attitudes and milieu of the Shire and even has a tattoo of its map. She is on gossiping terms with her neighbours, Brenda Bridgehead (insula), Felicity Feelall (thalamus) and her gym partner, Dudley Doit (motor cortex). When she is unwell, she can lose her sensitivity to her milieu and can become excessively preoccupied with her own appearance.

Reference

Ramachandran, V. and Blakeslee, S. (1999) *Phantoms in the Brain.* London: Fourth Estate.

Further reading

Castle, D. and Phillips, K. (eds) (2001) *Disorders of Body Image.* Philadelphia, PA: Wrightson Biomedical Publishing.
Ramachandran, V. (2003) *The Emerging Mind.* London: BBC/Profile Books.

Chapter 7

Maurice Mapply: the Parietal Lobes

Meet Maurice Mapply

Maurice lives south of the Great Divide (central sulcus) with Melissa Mirrorwood (somatosensory cortex). He has good friendships with his neighbours Fredrick Foresight (frontal lobe) and Rochelle Ringbond (cingulate gyrus), Lilly Listentale (temporal lobe), Penelope Panorama (occipital lobe) and Felicity Feelall (thalamus), but he is closest of all to Melissa. He loves her sensitivity and her body and they share a love of maps. Maurice is more aware than others of the world beyond Cephalton and the Shire. He has an extraordinary capacity to shift his focus back and forth from the big picture to the fine detail. In addition he is a truly skilled mathematician.

When Maurice is unwell he may be unaware of his illness and its impact upon those around. At these times he loses his ability to see the big picture and may become quite confused. On one occasion he was found wandering, unable to work out where he was, and unsure whether the coins in his pocket were the right ones to make a phone call. He could not even calculate whether he had sufficient money to take a taxi home.

The parietal lobes explained

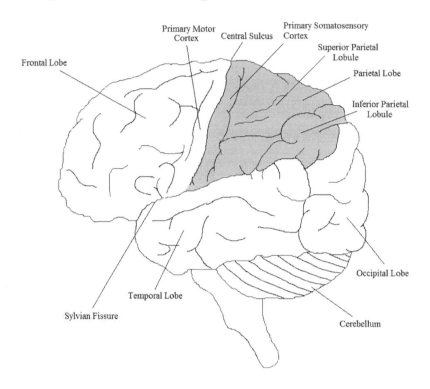

Figure 7.1. Lateral view (outer surface) of the left side of the brain showing the parietal lobe shaded in grey. Each of the main visible lobes of the brain is labelled.

Location and structure

The parietal lobes lie behind the frontal lobes, in front of the occipital lobes and above the temporal lobes. The parietal lobe consists of three parts: the somatosensory cortex (see Chapter 6) which forms its anterior border, the superior parietal lobule and the inferior parietal lobule.

Connections

The parietal lobe has connections with the frontal lobe and cingulate gyrus, the somatosensory cortex, the temporal lobe, the occipital lobes, the thalamus and the insula (see figure 7.2). It receives most of its input from the thalamus, with additional input from each of the other cortical areas, including the somatosensory cortex. Output is primarily to the frontal lobes and cingulate with additional output to the insula and occipital lobes.

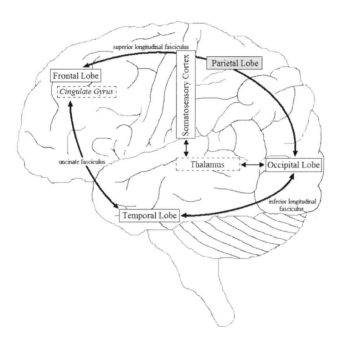

Figure 7.2. Lateral view (outer surface) of the left side of the brain, showing a schematic representation of the main connections of the parietal lobe with other key areas of the brain. Note the intimate connection between the thalamus, somatosensory cortex and parietal lobe.

Functions

The functions of the parietal lobe can be summarised as the 4As:

* Awareness of environment

* Attention

* Analysis of the environment.

* Arithmetical processing

AWARENESS OF ENVIRONMENT

A key function of the parietal lobe is the integration of information from the three main senses – visual, auditory and tactile – and consequently the construction of a comprehensive awareness of the environment. This includes visuospatial, auditory and tactile awareness and allows internal representation of the external world.

ATTENTION

Attention has four main components: selective, shifting, sustaining and supervisory. The parietal lobe is relevant to the first two. Selective attention involves focusing on specific aspects of the environment. Shifting attention is the transfer of focus from one aspect of the environment to another. These forms of attention enable the capturing of the most relevant components of the environment. The information is then relayed to the cingulate gyrus and frontal lobes for sustaining and supervising attention.

ANALYSIS OF THE ENVIRONMENT

This allows the answering of two main questions: what is it and where is it? Having established awareness and attention the parietal lobe clarifies the nature and location of the sensory stimuli.

ARITHMETICAL PROCESSING

This involves calculation and geometric reasoning. The parietal lobe allows the creative processing of symbols and shapes. This ability to represent aspects of our environment in terms of numbers and shapes allows us to deal accurately with general principles rather than treating each situation as a new experience. Put simply, this allows us, for example, to anticipate how many people we can carry in our car, rather than having to find out each time we want to carry passengers. It is intriguing that one of the greatest ever mathematicians, Einstein, had a significantly larger parietal lobe than normal, raising speculation that this may have contributed to his extraordinary mathematical skills.

In summary, the parietal lobes allow us to be aware, focused, analytical and creative. A common example involving all four functions is map-reading. We have to be aware of the environment, focus upon it and the map, analyse the detail, and use general principles to start planning our way.

When things go wrong

Parietal lobe dysfunction can manifest in five different ways corresponding to the four main functions.

IMPAIRMENT OF AWARENESS OF THE ENVIRONMENT

This may present as difficulties in integrating information from the three main senses, resulting in a lack of awareness of large parts of the environment. In extreme examples, such as stroke, tumour or trauma involving the posterior parietal lobe, victims may be completely unaware of half of their external world.

> Elsie, 82, who lived alone, had a fall and hit her head against the wall in her kitchenette. Although initially confused she was able to get up and put herself to bed. The following day she felt fine but three days later she was unable to get out of bed and was unaware that she was paralysed. Her

care worker who visited later that day noticed that Elsie had put only her right arm and not her left through her blouse, and seemed unaware of being only partially dressed. Investigations revealed a haemorrhage pressing onto the right parietal region.

The elderly are more prone to bleeding in or around the brain following trauma. Elsie's case illustrates that pathology affecting the parietal lobe can have major effects on awareness of the opposite side of the body to the trauma.

IMPAIRMENT OF ATTENTION

There are many forms of impairment of attention, of which some involve other parts of the brain. Problems affecting the parietal lobe are those relating to selective and shifting attention. Impairment of selective attention manifests as a tendency to focus on irrelevant aspects of the environment, rather than on those that are most relevant to the task in hand. Impairment of shifting attention presents as an inability to shift or a tendency to shift too readily.

> Alex, 14, had always been considered rather odd, especially because of his intense preoccupation with trains. His interest in every fine detail of train timetables, route maps, and location of stations took up all his spare time and formed the basis of all his conversation. He often failed to notice important things around him and had difficulty thinking about anything other than trains. In the classroom it was noted that he tended to live in a 'world of his own' and was unable to stay on task. On those few occasions when he was able to focus on other matters he lost his capacity to concentrate and became chaotic in his thinking. This pattern of behaviour had previously led to a diagnosis of attention deficit disorder but on the basis of his intense preoccupation with trains, to the exclusion of all else, more recently he had been diagnosed with Asperger's syndrome. Cognitive testing showed a normal IQ and verbal skills, but he had difficulty with attention and visuospatial skills.

Alex illustrates the various ways in which attention can be impaired when there is parietal lobe dysfunction. These include a tendency to focus on very fine detail at the cost of seeing the whole picture and the tendency to lose focus when attention is diverted from fine detail.

IMPAIRMENT OF ANALYSIS OF THE ENVIRONMENT

This can take two main forms: difficulties in establishing 'where' and difficulties in establishing 'what'. The former are manifested by impairment in directional sense and in finding one's way and the latter are manifested by an inability to recognise familiar objects even when examined by touch.

> Kenneth, 55, a highly respected author and professor of child psychiatry, had always surprised his friends by his total inability to recognise familiar landmarks and by the frequency with which he got lost, even when he was in his own neighbourhood. As time went by Kenneth found he couldn't even differentiate between objects in his pockets such as keys or coins. Neuropsychological testing revealed a score below the 3rd percentile for visuospatial memory.

Kenneth illustrates the spatial disorientation and inability to recognise objects (agnosia) experienced by many with impaired visuospatial skills due to parietal dysfunction.

IMPAIRMENT OF ARITHMETICAL PROCESSING

Many people have life-long difficulties in performing arithmetical calculations. In some this can be incapacitating and, as with the problems in analysis mentioned above, stands in contrast to the rest of their abilities.

> Lucy, 17, was entering her final year of secondary school. Despite her excellent grades in most of her subjects she performed very poorly in mathematics. Despite enormous effort and time she seemed unable to

grasp the basic concepts and continually made fundamental errors in calculation. Investigation of her school records by the educational psychologist revealed difficulties throughout her school career with a growing discrepancy between her mathematical performance and that of her peers. The psychologist advised Lucy and her parents that she should focus on those subjects not dependent upon arithmetical skills.

Undetected arithmetical difficulties are all too common and can lead to a false sense of general inadequacy. Parietal lobe dysfunction leading to difficulties of this sort can occur in the absence of any other impairments.

APRAXIA

The parietal lobe also plays an important role in motor skills. 'Apraxia' is the term used to describe the general loss of motor skills, when other causes of loss of motor skills have been excluded. Sufferers may try to initiate an activity that they would normally have done routinely and usually without effort, but then stop, declaring that they do not know how to perform it. Apraxia is often associated with lesions of the left parietal cortex.

Maurice Mapply in summary

Maurice lives in Midtown Cephalton with Melissa Mirrorwood and has a wide circle of friends. He is more aware than most of the world beyond Cephalton and its surrounds. His great loves are Melissa, maps and mathematics. When unwell he is unaware of his illness and its impact, has difficulty with attention, is prone to lose his way and unable to do the mathematics he loves so much.

Further reading

Gazzaniga, M.S., Ivry, R.B. and Mangun, G.R. (2007) *Cognitive Neuroscience: The Biology of the Mind*, 2nd edition. New York, NY: Norton.

Witelson, S.F., Kigar, D.L. and Harvey, T. (1999) 'The exceptional brain of Albert Einstein.' *Lancet 353*, 2149–2153.

Chapter 8

Penelope Panorama: the Occipital Lobes

Meet Penelope Panorama

Penelope lives behind Maurice Mapply's (parietal lobes) estate, in the south of Uptown Cephalton, above the estate of Frank Finesse (cerebellum). Although she is not one to talk, she is a very talented photographer with an amazing eye for detail. Penelope's skills mean she gives light and colour to every occasion in Cephalton. Her eye for balance, symmetry and analytical detail means that she is an invaluable advisor for any event and of course she is Cephalton's official photographer. Although photography is her forte she collects all art forms and files them, separating familiar from unfamiliar, personal from business, and monochrome from coloured. Once filed she then spends more time analysing them in detail.

Like so many of the other woman in Cephalton, she has always had an eye for Maurice Mapply (parietal lobes). She loves his big picture view and his capacity to appreciate her work. Despite this, she has a good working relationship with Maurice's partner, Melissa Mirrorwood (somatosensory cortex). Penelope's closest friends include Felicity Feelall (thalamus), her biggest supplier of artistic works and films, and Lilly Listentale (temporal lobes) who is constantly helping her with archiving and identifying artwork of interest. She also has a good day-to-day friendship with Fredrick Foresight, who directs and provides the final word for any exhibitions and master classes she may have, as well as with Sage Seahorse (hippocampus) and Annie Almond (amygdala).

Penelope usually keeps good health but her occasional ill health casts a cloud over the town. She has suffered from seizures which cause her to see things that she normally would not such as unusual shapes and scenes. She can experience severe headaches accompanied by seeing bright lights and zig zag lines. Sometimes she has been unable to make sense of what she is seeing.

The occipital lobes explained

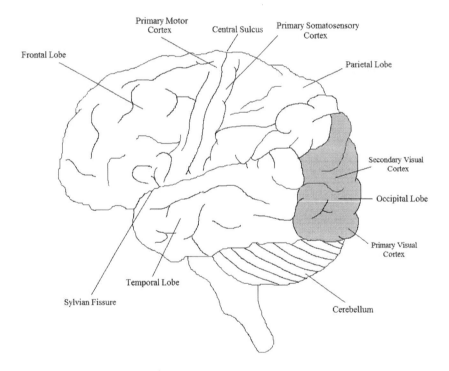

Figure 8.1. Lateral view (outer surface) of the left side of the brain showing the occipital lobe shaded in grey. Each of the main visible lobes of the brain is labelled.

Location and structure

The occipital lobe, the smallest of the four lobes of the brain, has the shape of a three-sided pyramid. It sits at the back of the brain, behind the parietal lobes and above the cerebellum. The main parts are the primary visual cortex on the medial side, and the secondary visual cortex, which is in turn divided into the lower visual association cortex, forming the bulk and the central core, and the higher visual association cortex, forming the anterolateral border.

Connections

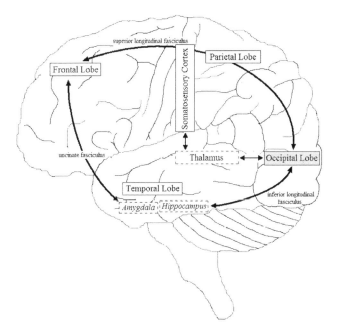

Figure 8.2. Lateral view (outer surface) of the left side of the brain, showing a schematic representation of the main connections of the occipital lobe with other key areas of the brain. Note the key roles of the superior longitudinal fasciculus ('the where pathway') and the inferior longitudinal fasciculus ('the what pathway'), which connect the occipital lobes to the parietal and temporal lobes respectively.

The occipital lobes receive input from the thalamus and relay information to the parietal lobes, the somatosensory cortex, the frontal lobes, the temporal lobes, hippocampus, and the amygdala.

Functions

The occipital lobe integrates and disseminates visual information. This works at four levels:

- The sensory level involves the reception of light
- The perceptual level involves the gathering together of this sensory information
- The interpretive level involves making sense of the information
- Dissemination involves relaying this integrated information to be brought to awareness (parietal lobe), combined with other sensory information (somatosensory cortex), past memories (hippocampus), working out what it is called (temporal lobe), and the current emotional state (amygdala)

All this information is relayed to and coordinated by the frontal lobes.

Taking as an example looking at a flower, light from the flower falls upon the retina, which sends a signal to the main sensory relay station (thalamus), which in turn relays the information to the occipital lobe (sensory component) in the primary visual cortex. From here it is sent to the lower visual association cortex for gathering of the information and then to the higher association cortex for interpretation (especially involving visual memory). Thus a flower is seen and recognised! Finally this information is relayed to the parietal lobe (spatial awareness), the somatosensory cortex (body awareness), the hippocampus (memory) and the amygdala (associated emotions).

When things go wrong

A number of problems may affect the occipital lobes.

SEIZURES

Seizures within the occipital lobe alone are uncommon. However, as part of a broader seizure picture within the brain as a whole they are more common. Seizures affecting the occipital lobe, and which produce visual symptoms such as hallucinations, are known as sensory or partial seizures. When other senses, e.g. olfactory or auditory, are involved they are known as complex partial seizures.

Occipital lobe seizures may produce visual symptoms at all four levels of function, e.g. at the *sensory* level, producing dots or zig zag lines; at the *perceptual* level, producing shapes and images and specific colours which are not actually related to what is within the visual field; at the *interpretive* level, producing complex visual experiences such as moving figures and important past figures; and at the *disseminative* level seizures may be associated with visuospatial abnormalities such as macropsia or micropsia (seeing things as larger or smaller than they usually are). Sensory integration abnormalities can occur, such as synaesthesia in which people 'see' sounds, 'taste' colours, and so on. Visual-affective experiences occur when people see normal visual images which are perceived as threatening.

Visual stimulation such as strobe lighting or dappled light may cause generalised seizures in predisposed individuals who have an occipital lobe abnormality such as scarring.

MIGRAINE

Migraine is a common form of headache, usually unilateral, commencing in childhood and associated with throbbing pain, often involving the eyes. It is due to fluctuations in blood flow to the occipital lobe and can produce simple visual hallucinations such as auras and flashing lights.

VISUAL HALLUCINATIONS

Hallucinations are sensory experiences without a sensory stimulus, but perceived as real, and occurring in any sensory modality. Visual hallucinations occur most commonly in the periods between wakeful-ness and sleep. The most common condition associated with visual hallucinations is delirium as, for example, in childhood febrile illness. These hallucinations are created by the response of occipital lobe cells, which would normally be stimulated by signals from the eye, firing inap-propriately as a result of insufficient oxygen or nutrients or in the presence of toxins.

VISUAL AGNOSIA

This involves the inability to recognise the meaning of what is seen. It occurs when the higher visual association cortex is unable to make sense of the visual stimuli, due to strokes, tumour, trauma or degenerative disease.

Technical corner: two types of vision

There are two linked systems for dealing with vision: conscious and unconscious. The conscious process, involving the connections between the eyes, the thalamus, the occipital lobes, the hippocampus, the amygdala, and the rest of the cortex, enables interpretation of visual information. The unconscious process, involving the eyes, the mid-brain, the thalamus and the motor cortex, enables a more rapid, reflex response to visual stimuli.

When the conscious process is disrupted by damage to the primary visual cortex (medial occipital lobes) this is known as cortical blindness. The reflex response (unconscious process) allows for what is known as 'blind-sight', in which there is an ability to respond reasonably accu-rately to a visual image despite seeming to be unable to see it.

Penelope Panorama in summary

Penelope Panorama lives in the southern part of Uptown Cephalton, close to Maurice Mapply (parietal lobe), Lilly Listentale (temporal lobe) and Frank Finesse (cerebellum). Her primary role is helping the community members to see what is happening beyond Cephalton. When she is unwell she may suffer seizures, migraine, hallucinations or more rarely be unable to make sense of what she sees (visual agnosia).

Further reading

Kandell, E.R., Schwartz, J.H. and Jessell, T.M. (2000) *Principles of Neural Science*, 4th edition. Sydney: McGraw-Hill.

Sabo, K.T. and Kirtley, D.D. (1982) 'Objects and activities in the dreams of the blind.' *International Journal of Rehabilitation Research 5*, 241–242.

Chapter 9

Lilly Listentale: the Temporal Lobes

Meet Lilly Listentale

Lilly Listentale lives in Uptown Cephalton. Her property borders on the outer edges of the Foresight Estate (frontal lobes) and the Mapply Estate (parietal lobes) and lies just north of the property of Penelope Panorama (occipital lobes). The northernmost part of her property sits near the Butterfly Cliffs (Sphenoidal Ridges), separating Uptown from Downtown Cephalton. There is a deep ravine running between the Foresight Estate and Lilly's place, known as the Sylvian Ravine (lateral or sylvian fissure).

Lilly is a great listener. She especially loves beautiful music and wonderful stories. She works at the Cephalton Conservatorium of Music and the Dramatic Arts, as a specialist archivist and audiovisual production consultant. But she does not just listen. She analyses and makes sense of music and audio productions in a way that no-one else can. She knows how to combine sound and visual media in a highly artistic, integrated and creative manner while being faithful to the reality of the artistic message. She is also a connoisseur of fine art and helps Penelope Panorama (occipital lobes) with her huge receiving house for artwork, photography and films. Her special interest in paintings is portraiture. The private collection of faces she has captured in portraits in various forms of media is nothing short of extraordinary.

Lilly's closest and oldest friends live nearby on her quite large property. Annie Almond (amygdala), Sage Seahorse (hippocampus) and Charles Chatterley (Wernicke's area) are all people she speaks to every day. She is especially close to Felicity Feelall (thalamus), the biggest supplier of music, artwork and wholesale raw material for art in Cephalton. She also listens to Penelope Panorama (occipital lobes), Maurice Mapply (parietal lobes) and Melissa Mirrorwood (somatosensory cortex). In turn, some very key people in Cephalton, such as Brenda Bridgehead (insula), Fredrick Foresight (frontal lobes) and Uma Underbride (hypothalamus), listen to her.

When Lilly is unwell life in Cephalton loses some of its music . She has been known to have times of total shutdown where she is deaf to the world around and nothing makes sense to her any more. At first people thought it was just her artistic temperament but in fact it was confirmed by medical tests that she has also had some seizures like her friend Penelope Panorama. These have led her to experience a sense of unreality, feeling cut off from others, with the familiar feeling unfamiliar and the unfamiliar familiar. She would see things smaller, larger or distorted from the way they usually and actually are. She would hear unusual sounds as if, for example, there was wind whistling through trees in her bedroom. Even though she could describe these as they happened, often she could not recall them later.

The temporal lobes explained

Location and structure

The temporal lobes are located beneath the frontal and parietal lobes, separated from them by the sylvian (or lateral) fissure, and in front of the occipital lobes. The temporal lobes sit immediately behind the wings of the sphenoid (Butterfly Cliffs). They consist of six main structures: the primary auditory cortex (superior temporal gyrus), the secondary auditory cortex (also in the superior temporal gyrus extending into the middle temporal gyrus), Wernicke's area, hippocampus, amygdala and fusiform gyrus. Given the importance and very specific functions of

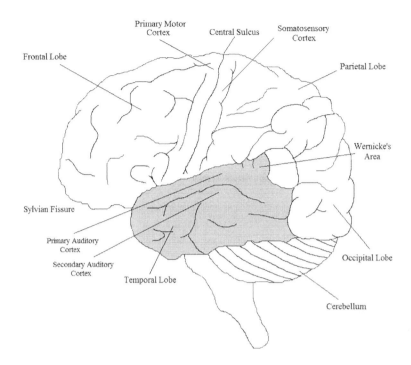

Figure 9.1. Lateral view (outer surface) of the left side of the brain showing the temporal lobe shaded in grey. Each of the main visible lobes of the brain is labelled.

Wernicke's area, the hippocampus and amygdala, we have devoted separate chapters to these structures. The fusiform gyrus is dealt with in this chapter as a classic case.

Connections

The connections need to be considered as those within the temporal lobe itself and those between the temporal lobe and other structures. Within the temporal lobe there are connections between the primary and secondary auditory cortex and Wernicke's area, fusiform gyrus, the amygdala and hippocampus. With regard to structures outside the temporal lobe there is direct input from the thalamus, the occipital, parietal and somatosensory cortex. In turn the temporal lobes relay information to the insula, the frontal lobes and the hypothalamus.

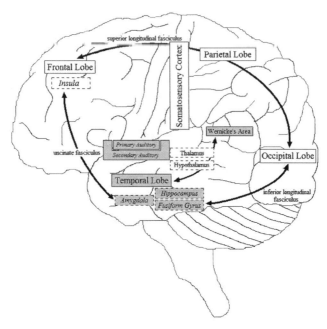

Figure 9.2. Lateral view (outer surface) of the left side of the brain, showing a schematic representation of the main connections of the temporal lobe with other key areas of the brain. Note the key roles of the interior longitudinal fasciculus ('the what pathway') and the uncinate fasciculus, connecting the occipital lobes and the frontal lobes respectively with the temporal lobes.

Functions

The predominant function of the temporal lobe is to integrate and disseminate auditory information, especially in relation to communication. This works at five levels: sensation, perception, interpretation, integration and dissemination. The temporal lobes:

- Integrate auditory information
- Interpret auditory information
- Disseminate auditory information

Sensation involves the reception of sound, perception the gathering together and packaging of this sensory information, and interpretation involves making sense of the information. Integration involves combining the auditory information with other information from the parietal lobe to allow for location, the somatosensory cortex for touch, occipital cortex for vision, hippocampus for past memories and amygdala for current emotional state. Dissemination involves relaying this integrated information to Broca's area and the rest of the frontal lobes.

Taking as an example listening to music, the sound falls upon the ear, which sends a signal to the main sensory relay station (thalamus) which in turn directs to the temporal lobe. Within the temporal lobe this auditory information is received by the primary auditory cortex, is then sent to the secondary lower auditory cortex, for gathering and packaging of the information, and then to the higher auditory cortex (Wernicke's area) for interpretation (especially involving auditory memory). Thus the music is heard and recognised! This is then combined with information from the parietal lobe (location), the somatosensory cortex (association with touch), the hippocampus to enable memories for previous music, and the amygdala for the associated emotional tone.

When things go wrong

In this section we only discuss the auditory components of the temporal lobe as the impact on Wernicke's area, the hippocampus and the amygdala are all dealt with in separate chapters. The temporal lobes can be affected by many different conditions, occurring from the prenatal period through to old age. These include prenatal infection, seizures, trauma, stroke and dementias.

PRENATAL INFECTION

Infection with rubella virus in the first 16 weeks of pregnancy can affect the development of the primary auditory cortex with the potential for consequent deafness.

SEIZURES

There are many causes of seizures in the temporal lobes because of their vulnerability to injury and insult before and after birth. Characteristics of seizures specific to the temporal lobe (known as complex partial seizures or temporal lobe epilepsy) include déjà vu, jamais vu, seeing things as larger or smaller than their real size (macropsia or micropsia), and complex hallucinations involving multiple sensory components, and extreme emotions, such as intense rage, fear or pleasure.

> Billy, aged 14, had experienced a difficult birth with a prolonged second stage of labour. His developmental milestones were delayed and he had difficulties with school work. Spoken instructions caused him particular problems. Despite anticonvulsant medication he experienced seizures every two to three weeks which had the same basic pattern. They would start shortly after waking when he would call out in fear and would huddle in a corner calling out repetitively that he was being attacked. Occasionally after a couple of minutes he would have a typical grand-mal seizure. Afterwards he would remember nothing and remained sleepy and confused for several hours. In between these major seizures he would have unusual episodes when he would insist he was somewhere he had never been and at other times seeming not to recognise places with which he was normally familiar. Also he would experience others as reducing or increasing in size for brief periods of time and occasionally he would tell his mother that he felt strange and that things did not seem real.

Billy illustrates a history of damage at the time of birth to the temporal lobes with consequent learning difficulties, particularly relating to the spoken word. The behaviour is characteristic of complex partial seizures with the preceding emotional arousal and accompanying hallucinations, with occasional grand-mal seizures.

TRAUMA

When the temporal lobe is traumatised, hearing can be impaired due to damage to the primary auditory cortex. Difficulties making sense of what is heard may occur as a result of damage to the secondary auditory cortex.

STROKE

When the blood supply to the temporal lobes is interrupted, difficulties in all components of hearing may occur.

> Elisabeth, 57, had suffered from hypertension for ten years and had a family history of heart disease. During a meeting at work she seemed to become self-absorbed and unable to hear what others were saying to her. When asked if she was okay she looked puzzled and responded irrelevantly. She was taken to hospital and found to have extremely high blood pressure and a haemorrhage in the left temporal lobe. Subsequently she made a slow recovery, with persistent difficulty in making sense of what she was hearing. A hearing test showed no abnormalities.

This case illustrates how a stroke localised to the auditory cortex can be quite disabling even after recovery from the initial episode. Elisabeth continued to have problems with auditory discrimination, leading to each individual word she heard being less distinct. This is due to dysfunction in the secondary auditory cortex.

DEMENTIA

The impact of dementia on the temporal lobe is widespread, with the most notable effect, other than on the hippocampus, being on the secondary auditory cortex with loss of understanding of what is heard.

The classic temporal lobes case: the man who mistook his wife for a hat

The most famous case of temporal lobe disturbance was that described by Oliver Sacks (1986). Dr P. was a distinguished musician and teacher who became unable to recognise his students when they approached him, but could identify them once they spoke. He then began turning his ears towards people when meeting with them and would 'see' faces in other things such as the top of water-hydrants or in pieces of furniture. Also he could not recognise pictures of his family, except if they had a very distinct facial feature such as a square jaw. On one occasion, as if intending to put on his hat, he reached toward his wife's head, which he had mistaken for his hat. On testing he showed no problems with vision although he appeared to have difficulty in interpreting visual information. He showed no other signs of dementia. Dr P. suffered from prosopagnosia, a failure to recognise familiar faces, due to damage to the fusiform gyrus, the role of which is to link recognition with facial visual stimuli.

Technical corner

A highly specialised aspect of auditory processing is that relating to hearing foreign languages. The perception and integration of such language occurs in a specific aspect of the primary auditory cortex known as Heschl's gyrus, situated on the surface of the superior temporal gyrus. Neuroimaging has shown that subjects who have no difficulty learning a foreign language have a larger Heschl's gyrus than those who do have such difficulty.

Bryan is an ageing but very active, energetic and reasonably intelligent child psychiatrist and author. He is extremely well travelled, having lived abroad and visited every continent many times. Although he can just about manage to read and write in one or two foreign languages, he is completely unable to understand their spoken words. He also struggles to speak in another language even though he can understand many written words of that language. He insists he does not need any brain imaging to prove that he has an almost microscopic Heschl's gyrus. As sufferers of this affliction receive mockery rather than sympathy, he has decided to give the condition the recognition he believes it deserves by providing it with a name: idiopathic dys-xenolingua (inability to converse in foreign languages – cause unknown).

Lilly Listentale in summary

Lilly Listentale lives in Midtown Cephalton and is close friends and neighbours with Charles Chatterley, Sage Seahorse and Annie Almond. She is a great listener, especially to Felicity Feelall, Penelope Panorama, Maurice Mapply and Melissa Mirrorwood. In turn, key people such as Brenda Bridgehead, Fredrick Foresight and Uma Underbride listen to her. She is very artistic, especially in relation to all matters relating to sound and vision. She loves her very special, private collection of portraits. When she is unwell she can have seizures and has even been affected by a stroke.

Further reading

Gazzaniga, M.S., Ivry, R.B. and Mangun, G.R. (2007) *Cognitive Neuroscience: The Biology of the Mind*, 2nd edition. New York, NY: Norton.

Reading, J.P. and Will, R.G. (1997) 'Unwelcome orgasms.' *The Lancet 350*, 1746.

Sacks, O. (1986) *The Man who Mistook his Wife for a Hat*. London: Picador.

Chapter 10

Brenda Bridgehead: the Insula

Meet Brenda Bridgehead

Brenda Bridgehead, Cephalton's richest landowner and leading philanthropist, lives in a very secluded hideaway in the deepest part of Sylvian Ravine (sylvian fissure) with property extending up to the Foresight Estate (frontal lobes). Her property overhangs, and falls on either side of, Corrie O'Graphie's (basal ganglia) place, while bordering at Midtown on the huge Mapply (parietal lobes), Listentale (temporal lobes) and Mirrorwood (somatosensory cortex) Estates.

The two main parts of her properties – the Eastern and Western triangles (right and left insulae)   are connected by the access road across Frontbridge (anterior commisure) on Christopher Crosstalk's (corpus callosum) property. Many 'in the know' among estate agents believe it is one of the best locations, and best-kept secrets, in Cephalton. It is not simply that she has a large property – after all others are much larger – it is much more about its location and communication links.

Brenda is able to name among her contacts more people, from different parts of Cephalton, with more diverse backgrounds, than anyone else. Very many of the key people in Cephalton live near her and each has a quite different but special relationship with her. On first impressions, Brenda is out of the public eye, living away from the hurley burley of everyday life and politics. Most people are not at all sure what she does or where she lives. But a closer inspection reveals that Brenda can and does mix with the most prominent and influential people, while still not losing the common touch with the lesser-known and largely unchronicled Cephalton lives and personalities. She has business and social relationships with almost all the key cliques and factions in town.

She has excellent taste, especially for good cuisine. Although she listens to the editor of the Cephalton Good Food Guide and food critic, Tim Tickertaste (nucleus of the solitary tract), she makes the final call on the menu for all public occasions. Her memory for when someone served something bad is legendary; no-one can 'do disgust' better than Brenda and she can recognise the same in other people, even when they try to disguise it. Through her close friendship with Felicity Feelall, Brenda feels the pain of the whole community in a quite visceral way and is one of the most empathic figures in Cephalton. She played the driving role in getting the Cephalton Hospital built Downtown just beyond Lake Tertius (third ventricle) with one of the first specialised pain units run by her hero and current love, Dr Ernie Enkephalin (periaqueductal grey matter). She has been in relationships with Sage Seahorse (hippocampus), Fredrick Foresight (frontal lobes) and Maurice Mapply (parietal lobes), all of whom continue to find her a very attractive and deeply sensual person. Surprisingly, this has not stopped her from having close friendships with their partners, Annie Almond (amygdala), Rochelle Ringbond (cingulate gyrus) and Melissa Mirrorwood (somatosensory cortex).

Her friends, Annie Almond, Uma Underbride (hypothalamus) and Rosie Reaction (autonomic nervous system), might do 'fright, flight and fight' in response to a community threat, but Brenda's is the voice of calm – her mantra is 'rest and digest'. She apprises Fredrick Foresight of the 'guts of the issues' facing Cephalton and its surrounds, and eases the pain when someone gets hurt. When hearts are racing, she calms things down and encourages reflection. She is a deeply stabilising influence and very good at conveying to the community how things really are.

Brenda is a truly complex person and despite, or perhaps because of, the good she does for everyone, she can have her own problems. She can become quiet and introspective, taking on other people's pain and shame. When someone else is in pain, Brenda feels it. In particular, when Melissa considers herself fat or ugly, Brenda feels her self-disgust. She may stop eating or drinking and can no longer enjoy the normal pleasures of life. She finds it difficult to make sense of her feelings and cannot help the community to maintain its normal 'balance'. Indeed, she shuts off from those around her.

The insula explained

Location and structure

The insula is the fifth major cortical lobe, often overlooked because, unlike the others, it is not on the brain's surface. It is a triangular-shaped structure, so named because it looks like an island. Located in the Sylvian fissure, the insula lies inferior to the frontal lobes, medial to the temporal lobes and anterior to the parietal lobes. It has two major parts, anterior and posterior.

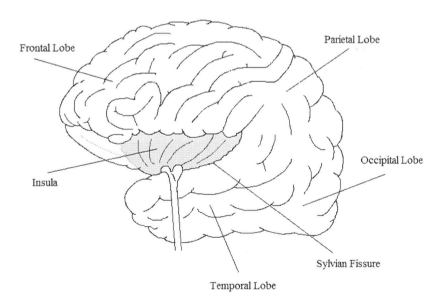

Figure 10.1. Lateral view (outer surface) of the left side of the brain showing the insular cortex shaded in grey. Each of the main lobes of the brain is labelled.

Connections

The insula's connections (and functions) are so many that it is easy to become overwhelmed by their complexity. In brief there are connections with: the frontal lobes (Fredrick Foresight), including Broca's area (Cherry Chatterley), the cingulate gyrus (Rochelle Ringbond), the temporal lobes (Lilly Listentale), including Wernicke's area (Charles Chatterley), the amygdala (Annie Almond), and the hippocampus (Sage Seahorse), the parietal lobes (Maurice Mapply), the somatosensory cortex (Melissa Mirrorwood), the basal ganglia (Corrie O'Graphie), the thalamus (Felicity Feelall), the hypothalamus (Uma Underbride), the periaqueductal grey matter (Dr Ernie Enkephalin), the pons and medulla (Fay Faceandear and Sam Swallowtalk), and the nucleus of the solitary tract (Tim Tickertaste).

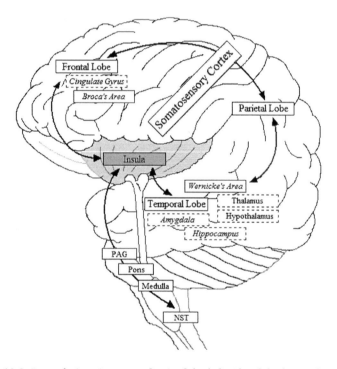

Figure 10.2. Lateral view (outer surface) of the left side of the brain showing the main connections of the insula with other key areas of the brain. PAG = periaqueductal grey matter; NST = nucleus tractus solitarius = nucleus of the solitary tract.

In fact the only major parts of the brain that have no direct contact with the insula are the occipital lobes (Penelope Panorama), the pituitary (Horace Hormone) and the cerebellum (Frank Finesse).

Functions

Just as the insula's connections are highly complex so are its functions. It is a bridge between the right and left sides of the brain, between the feeling brain and the thinking brain and between the expression and reception of speech and emotions. The insula can in a sense be compared to an internet server, which has the potential to facilitate communication between millions of people. Similarly, the insula facilitates and regulates communication between the millions of brain cells in the various structures to which it is connected.

The predominant role of the insula is to orchestrate the balance between those parts of the brain that deal with adaptation to the external environment and those responsible for internal homeostasis. It does this through a number of subsidiary functions (see Table 10.1), the majority of which relate to its role as a network of connections.

REGULATION OF THE AUTONOMIC NERVOUS SYSTEM

The higher functions of the brain often act as a brake upon lower functions, much as parents do with their children. The insula serves a similar function, when necessary, by acting as a brake upon the amygdala and its major outflow to the sympathetic nervous system and by acting as a central stimulator of the parasympathetic nervous system.

REGULATION OF APPETITE AND EATING

When hungry and before eating there is increased activity in the insula. This diminishes after eating, reflecting its central role in communication about appetite between the frontal lobes and the hypothalamus. Key functions of the insula are:

- Balancing external adaptation with internal homeostasis

- Regulation of the autonomic nervous system

- Regulation of appetite and eating

- Taste and visceral memory

- Monitoring of the body state

- Integration of thoughts and feelings

- Provision of investment of emotion to language

- Regulation of the experience of pain

- Experience of disgust

TASTE AND VISCERAL MEMORY

The insula is the major site for the reception, perception and integration of taste and for visceral memories. It links taste to the memory of various foods, and might even be considered as the hippocampus (contextual memory) for the gut. These functions are closely linked with the regulation of appetite and eating.

MONITORING OF THE BODY STATE

As a bridge between the frontal lobes (conscious thought), the somatosensory cortex (body image) and the visceral feedback system from inner organs (of, for example, the senses of pain, distension or pleasure) the insula provides experience of 'how my body is'. Also, through its connection between the frontal and parietal lobes, the insula provides awareness of 'the world around my body'.

INTEGRATION OF THOUGHTS AND FEELINGS

The insula links the frontal lobes, which are prominent in all matters to do with conscious thought, to the limbic system, specifically the amygdala and the cingulate gyrus, which are concerned with feelings relating to threat, affection and attachment. These connections allow for a linking of thoughts with feelings.

PROVISION OF INVESTMENT OF EMOTION TO LANGUAGE

The insula connects the specialised speech centres (Broca's area for expression and Wernicke's area for reception), adding clarity of speech, emotional tone and nuance (prosody). This is illustrated by brain scanning in dyslexia. In non-dyslexic people, when conducting word tasks, there is increased activity in both the speech centres and in the insula. In those with dyslexia, however, the insula does not show increased activity; rather each language area appears to function separately. The insula links the language areas and orchestrates their activity.

REGULATION OF THE EXPERIENCE OF PAIN

By connecting the thalamus with the somatosensory and frontal lobes the insula is central to relaying the sensation of pain. This allows the frontal lobes to respond with appropriate defensive strategies and for messages also to be sent to the periaqueductal grey matter which in turn sends messages via the spinal cord, over-riding, blocking or reducing pain signals. For example, whilst involved in sport, an injury may occur, the pain from which is not experienced till after the event. In contrast, when picking up a hot plate without the realisation that it is hot, the pain is experienced immediately. In each case the insula is regulating the experience of pain.

EXPERIENCE OF DISGUST

Unlike all its other functions, which are based on the insula connecting other centres, this function is intrinsic to the insula. There are two components: primary disgust – an emotional experience (for example, the reaction to a nauseating smell or sight), and secondary disgust – a learned experience (for example, having previously eaten some food that was 'off' that led to a stomach upset, the next time such food is encountered the nausea experienced is a reaction of secondary disgust). Both processes involve the insula, the primary being mediated by the anterior portion, and the secondary via the ventrolateral portion.

In summary, at the simplest level the insula is a pivotal structure in permitting adaptation of the organism to the external environment.

When things go wrong

The actual site of any dysfunction within the insula would be critical in determining symptoms. An abnormality at one site in such a complex of connections would have very different effects from an abnormality at another site.

ANOREXIA NERVOSA

In anorexia nervosa there are abnormalities in the regulation of appetite and eating, an exaggerated sense of fullness, distortion of body image, difficulties in the integration of thoughts and feelings, anosognosia (unawareness of being ill) and a heightened sense of disgust. These are all compatible with impairment of insula function. The cognitive deficits commonly noted in anorexia nervosa, specifically impairments in executive functioning and visuospatial processing, could be explained by a dysfunction within the network of connections around the insula.

> Amy, 15, is preoccupied by the wish to be thinner and better toned. She has a marked fear of weight gain and will go to extreme measures to ensure that this does not occur. She first became concerned about her appearance at age 12, when her dance teacher commented on her weight. Worried that she would be too fat to dance, Amy began restricting her food to the point of eating nothing that contained fat and regularly skipped meals. She started running 5 km in the morning and swimming 100 laps each afternoon on top of her already busy dance schedule. She would weigh herself many times a day and constantly compare herself to other girls her age to see if she had gained any weight. Although she was

aware of feeling tired and irritable she continued with her strict diet and exercise regimen.

Amy often felt bloated and fat after eating small amounts of food and felt overwhelmingly disgusted with herself and her body. In consequence she would purge and/or exercise straight after eating. She began to sleep more and due to her fatigue started dropping in her grades at school. This upset Amy greatly as she was not happy with anything less than a perfect performance in all aspects of her life. Eventually she collapsed at school and required hospitalisation. On admission she was found to have a very low pulse rate, to be dehydrated and hypothermic with a temperature of 35 °C.

All the core features of anorexia nervosa plus the commonly associated cognitive deficits could be accounted for by impairment of insula function.

EPILEPSY

Seizures that affect the insula have phenomena in common with seizures affecting other parts of the brain. However, they are also commonly associated with gastrointestinal sensations such as strange tastes, nausea, abdominal discomfort, vomiting and pain. They can be treatment-resistant and also difficult to investigate because of the depth of the insula within the brain.

STROKE

One of the most mysterious aspects of damage to the right insula is the tendency to be unaware of something that is radically wrong with the body (anosognosia). For example, people who have a right-hemisphere stroke are often paralysed on the left but if the stroke involves the insula they may not realise that they are paralysed and may attempt, for example, to get out of bed. This unawareness of there being something wrong is sometimes seen by others as 'denial' but it is firmly rooted in organic pathology.

Brenda Bridgehead in summary

Brenda Bridgehead (insula), despite living deep in the Sylvian Ravine, is one of the key figures in the life of Cephalton and is one of the best-connected people there. She is attuned to the community's pain and emotions and has her own strong gut feelings. She can calm the situation when feelings are strong but is also able to show her disgust when the situation provokes it. When she is unwell she can become depressed, disgusted by her body, nauseous, have gastrointestinal discomfort or pain, eat much less than normal, and lose weight.

Further reading

Brizendine, L. (2006) *The Female Brain*. New York, NY: Broadway Books.

Nunn, K., Lask, B., Frampton, I. and Gordon, I. (2008 submitted) '"The fault, Horatio, is not in her parents, but in her insula" – a neurobiological hypothesis to explain the core clinical features of anorexia nervosa.'

Shelley, B. and Trimble, M. (2004) 'The insular lobe of Reil – its anatomico-functional, behavioural and neuropsychiatric attributes in humans.' *Biological Psychiatry 5*, 176–200.

Part Three
The Subcortex

Chapter 11

Christopher Crosstalk: the Corpus Callosum

Meet Christopher Crosstalk

The 'Gentle Giant of Cephalton', Christopher Crosstalk (corpus callosum) lives right in the centre of town, neatly dividing East and West Cephalton. His property stretches from Uptown right through to the lower end of Midtown with neighbours such as Rochelle Ringbond (cingulate gyrus) at one end, and Penelope Panorama (occipital lobes) and Maurice Mapply (parietal lobes) at the other. The huge Crosstalk Estate lies near the Twin Great Lakes (lateral ventricles) and skirts much of Lake Tertius (third ventricle), where Felicity Feelall (thalamus) lives.

Christopher is possibly the most public minded of all the inhabitants of Cephalton. He allows everyone to cross his property to get quickly across town. Indeed, he has more traffic across his land than any other road in Cephalton – public or private – and he is very sociable, talking to everyone. He is not just a town gossip. He is a real institution. Everyone knows that, without him, Cephalton would be a divided community – two towns instead of one, living parallel existences. It would also mean there would have to be much more duplication of town resources with, for example, theatres, swimming pools and shopping malls on both sides of town.

If Christopher Crosstalk became severely ill then the bridges and tunnel on his land would no longer run smoothly. Fortunately, however, most things would go on as usual. What would change is the cooperation between both sides of town on difficult and complex projects. Everyone would gradually notice that the specialty shops and services would not be able to maintain their high standard and most places would have to have more general goods and services. It would be as if there were two towns. In fact, almost always at least one of the crossings remains open. Strangely, sometimes during crises, especially electrical storms (epilepsy), there can be advantages to Christopher being away, sick or unavailable. If power goes out on one side of the town, it does not spread to the other if the two sides of town are disconnected. Any problem that can be isolated to one side of the town can be contained.

The corpus callosum explained

Location and structure

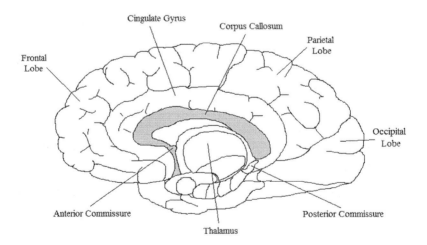

Figure 11.1. Medial view (inner surface) of the right side of the brain showing the corpus callosum with the three sections labelled. Each of the main visible lobes of the brain is labelled.

The corpus callosum is a very thick midline bundle of nerve fibres that connects the left and right hemispheres of the brain. The corpus callosum is the largest single nerve tract system, consisting of around 200–250 million fibres. It sits just above the thalamus and third ventricle and immediately below the cingulate gyrus.

There are three connecting bundles:

1. The anterior commissure, inferior to the lateral ventricles

2. The body of the corpus callosum, crossing above the third ventricle

3. The posterior commissure (splenium), bridging the two parietal lobes and the two occipital lobes

Women tend to have a larger corpus callosum in proportion to total brain size, presumably facilitating greater communication between the hemispheres, although debate has been lively on this point.

Connections

The corpus callosum, along with the smaller anterior commissure and the splenium posteriorly, allow all the major structures of the brain to be connected to their counterpart on the other side. In fact there are three types of connections:

1. Connections between the right and left hemisphere with parts of the cortex that do *similar tasks*

2. Connections between the right and left hemispheres with parts of the cortex that do *different tasks*

3. Connections *within* each hemisphere, in which fibres from the corpus callosum on one side reach out to areas in the cortex of the same side

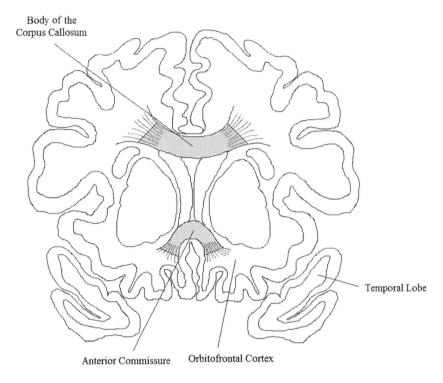

Body of the
Corpus Callosum

Temporal Lobe

Anterior Commissure   Orbitofrontal Cortex

Figure 11.2. Coronal (cross section of the brain from the front) view of the frontal lobes of the brain, showing the corpus callosum connecting the right and left sides of the brain.

Functions

The corpus callosum has three main functions:

- Allows communication between hemispheres
- Allows specialisation among the hemispheres
- Allows communication within the hemispheres

ALLOWS THE TWO HALVES OF THE BRAIN TO COMMUNICATE WITH EACH OTHER

This provides for communication, cooperation, and sometimes competition, between the two sides of the brain. Specifically, the corpus callosum enables transfer of: (a) motor information to assist coordination between the two sides of the body; (b) auditory information to enhance meaning; (c) visuospatial information to provide awareness; and (d) transfer of multiple sensory modality information to provide integrated experiences and consciousness.

These transfers between each half of the brain linking neurons, performing very different roles, enable higher order integrative experiences. For example, when recognising, interpreting and responding to facial expression in others there is an elaborate integration of sound, sight and movement of both hemispheres with the right hemisphere more often contributing to understanding tone of voice, intention and gesture, and the left hemisphere making sense of the meaning of words and sequence of what is happening.

ALLOWS THE TWO HALVES OF THE BRAIN TO SPECIALISE

There is a division of labour and functions within the brain (see Table 11.1 below) which is dependent upon the integrity of the corpus callosum.

ALLOWS THE TRANSFER OF INFORMATION WITHIN THE SAME HEMISPHERE

The binding together of experiences into consciousness so that the five senses are in synchrony with each other is dependent upon communication within, as well as between, each hemisphere.

When things go wrong

When the corpus callosum is affected by conditions such as epilepsy, stroke, tumours and multiple sclerosis, information may not be transferred between different parts of the brain, and especially between the two hemispheres.

EPILEPSY AND SPLIT-BRAIN PATIENTS

The severing of the corpus callosum is used in severe epilepsy to prevent seizures crossing from one hemisphere to the other in order to ensure that only one side of the body is affected. Strangely the seizures not only fail to spread but also usually become less frequent. Those who undergo such surgery, or experience other damage to the corpus callosum, usually maintain their intellect, motivation and coordination. Initially after the surgical severing of the corpus callosum, the hemispheres act like separate people sharing the one body. For example, one split-brain person repeatedly took items from the grocery shelf with one hand and then returned them with the other (Reuter-Lorenz and Miller 1998). While the severed halves of the corpus callosum do not grow back together, the brain learns to use the other smaller connections between the left and right hemispheres (Myers and Sperry 1985).

> Philip, a 30-year-old male had had his corpus callosum severed six months previously, due to the frequency and severity of his seizures. His neurologist and neurosurgeon advised him that the operation would help keep the seizures in his left hemisphere where they originated and might in fact decrease their frequency in general. The surgery was a success with regards to controlling the seizures. Philip has, however, experienced some less obvious consequences of such surgery. For example, when undergoing testing with a cognitive psychologist, he was presented with words on either side of a screen. When a word was shown on the right of the screen, he was able to read it aloud but when the same words were shown on the left of the screen, he was unable to do so. However, he could still identify non-verbally the objects that matched those words.

The reason that Philip could pronounce the words when they appeared on the right of the screen is because this information is received in the left hemisphere, dominant for speech. However, when the words appeared on the left hand side of the screen, the information is received in the right (non-verbal) hemisphere, allowing Philip to respond non-verbally but not verbally.

AGENESIS OF THE CORPUS CALLOSUM

The congenital absence (partial or complete) of the corpus callosum (ACC) is a rare birth defect (in around one in 3000 births), occurring as a result of damage to the developing foetus within the first ten to eleven weeks of gestation. If the damage occurs later than ten weeks of gestation, the anterior commissure is often spared. People with ACC may manage many tasks as the two hemispheres have 'learned' to compensate for the lack of connection between each other; for example, they are not dependent upon the specialisation of each hemisphere.

> Jane, aged seven, was diagnosed with ACC while in utero following an ultrasound. Since the age of two she had had seizures, as well as feeding problems and appeared delayed in holding her head erect, sitting, standing and walking. Jane also appeared clumsy and to have poor motor coordination. Recent neuropsychological testing showed her to be of normal intelligence. Her treatment consisted of anti-epileptic medication to prevent her from having seizures.

Technical corner

Although all brain functions occur on both sides, the two hemispheres specialise in different areas – in other words more emphasis on a particular function occurs on one side than the other. For example, the right hemisphere specialises in emotional analysis and the left in logical analysis. The different emphases are then integrated and supported by the corpus callosum to produce a unified sense of consciousness. Table 11.1 shows the differences in emphasis between the two sides.

Table 11.1. Differences in emphasis in specialisation between the two hemispheres which are integrated and supported by the corpus callosum to produce a unified sense of consciousness

Left hemisphere	Right hemisphere
Awareness of time	Awareness of space
Awareness of fine detail	Awareness of big picture
Single tasks	Multi-tasking
Logical analysis	Emotional analysis
Production and comprehension of the words of speech	Production and comprehension of the emotions of speech
Expression of positive emotion	Expression of negative emotion
Activation of behaviour – approach	Inhibition of behaviour – with-drawal

Christopher Crosstalk in summary

Few in Cephalton are such strong communicators as Christopher Crosstalk (corpus callosum). He has enabled the community to be diverse and sophisticated and to divide tasks and projects up in a way that shares the load between both halves of town. He has also enabled different people on the same side of town to communicate more effectively. Life on the two sides of Cephalton can survive without Christopher and the access roads and crossings on his property. However, there is a definite loss of specialisation across the town when this loss occurs. Sometimes during crises, especially electrical storms (epilepsy), there can be advantages to Christopher being out of action, as the problem is isolated to one side of the town.

References

Myers, J.J. and Sperry, R.W. (1985) *Interhemisphere Communication After Section of the Forebrain Commissures Cortex 21*, 249–260.

Reuter-Lorenz, P.A. and Miller, A.C. (1998) 'The cognitive neuroscience of human laterality: Lessons from the bisected brain' *Current Directions in Psychological Science 7*, 15–20.

Further reading

Carter, R. (2002) *Mapping the Mind.* London: Phoenix.

Gazzaniga, M.S. and LeDoux, J.E. (1978) *The Integrated Mind.* New York, NY: Plenum Press.

Chapter 12

Sage Seahorse: the Hippocampus

Meet Sage Seahorse

Sage is one of the New Breed, like those in Uptown Cephalton, but lives in Midtown Cephalton to be closer to the activity of town life. He lives on Lilly Listentale's estate. He has attracted salacious gossip because of his relationship with the younger and very passionate Annie Almond (amygdala), who lives next door, just north of him.

Like his good friend and rival, Fredrick Foresight, he is a big picture person and able to grasp new situations and their significance very quickly. But whilst Fredrick sees the big picture at any one moment, Sage sees it over time and can put everything into a historical perspective. He always remembers times, places and names, having a keen sense of history and all things past. He knows more of the history of Cephalton than anyone and is the obvious choice for his position as President of the Historical Society.

Sage is a calm person who never panics, and whenever possible, stops others from panicking. He keeps people focused on the relevant issues and reminds them of past times and places, both positive and negative. Annie Almond (amygdala) and Uma Underbride (hypothalamus) make sure that he is never far from any crisis that touches the town as a whole. His friends include Felicity Feelall (thalamus) and his very wealthy uncle Al Zheimer (nucleus of Meynert). They all meet up regularly for coffee.

Sage draws enormous strength from Felicity's sensitivity and is refreshed by Al's appreciation of the past. At the same time Sage also keeps in touch with the town leadership, especially Fredrick Foresight (frontal lobes).

When Sage is unwell he forgets facts he normally knows so well and becomes disoriented, unable to absorb new information or to keep the Historical Society archives in order. He is easily upset.

The hippocampus explained

Location and structure

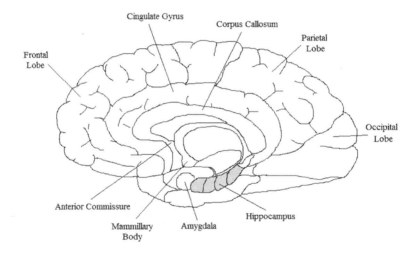

Figure 12.1. Medial view (inner surface) of the right side of the brain showing the hippocampus. Each of the main visible lobes of the brain is labelled.

The hippocampus is actually the inferomedial part of the temporal lobe (see Chapter 9) and lies in the floor of the lateral ventricle, close to the amygdala. The hippocampus is composed of three parts: the dentate gyrus, Ammon's horn and the subiculum. It is so called because its appearance is somewhat reminiscent of a seahorse. The hippocampus is usually larger in women than in men.

Connections

The hippocampus has reciprocal connections with the frontal lobe, the thalamus, the hypothalamus, the amygdala and the nucleus of Meynert.

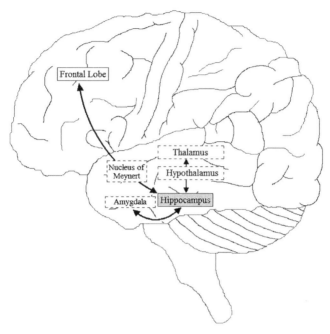

Figure 12.2. Lateral view (outer surface) of the left side of the brain showing schematic representation of the connections of the hippocampus. Note the intimate relationship between the amygdala (emotions) and the hippocampus (personal conscious, contextual memory).

Functions

The hippocampus has four main functions in relation to learning and memory:

- New learning
- Contextual memory
- Declarative memory
- Linking emotion to memory

NEW LEARNING

Unlike the cells of most other parts of the brain the cells of the hippo-campus are able to reproduce, thus allowing for new learning. Hence the hippocampus is the centre for new learning. This is illustrated by the fact that the hippocampus of a London taxi driver, who needs to have a truly encyclopaedic knowledge of London's streets before he can receive a license, is larger than that of people working in other professions (McGuire, Frackowiak and Firth 1997).

CONTEXTUAL MEMORY

The hippocampus is involved in establishing the background or context for each situation and memory. It plays an important function in the sense of location, situation and memory for places.

CONSCIOUS (DECLARATIVE) MEMORY

Sometimes, when asked to do certain tasks, people may not '*know* that they know but can *show* that they know'. The hippocampus, however, gives conscious knowledge to knowing – declarative memory.

LINKING EMOTION TO MEMORY

Through its intimate relationship with the amygdala, and consequently other parts of the limbic system, the hippocampus plays an important role in the relationship between emotion and memory, i.e. the emotions created by specific memories and the memories triggered by certain emotions.

When things go wrong

Hippocampus function can be profoundly affected by stress, depression, head injury, herpes encephalitis and dementia.

NEW LEARNING IMPAIRED BY STRESS

The stress hormone, cortisol, which is raised in severe depression and at times of anxiety, appears to inhibit memory, possibly due to increased vulnerability of hippocampal cells and subsequent destruction. In turn, hippocampal damage can lead to increased cortisol levels, causing a vicious cycle to develop. Older people, who generally have high cortisol levels, tend to be those with the smallest hippocampus and the greatest memory difficulties. Also it has been suggested that post-traumatic stress disorder (PTSD) victims have a smaller than average hippocampus, possibly due to raised cortisol levels. Alternatively the size difference might have preceded the trauma and rendered the victim more vulnerable to PTSD.

CONTEXTUAL AND CONSCIOUS MEMORY AFFECTED BY DEMENTIA

Alzheimer's disease is associated with widespread atrophy of a number of brain areas, including the hippocampus and the cerebral cortex.

> Ray, 65, had led a productive life raising a family and working in several important jobs. He enjoyed painting and had won a number of competitions for his artwork. A few years after retirement he noticed that he kept forgetting where he put things around the house such as his car keys. He would also forget important dates, such as birthdays and doctors appointments, and even what he had just done. His memory gradually deteriorated further and sometimes he found himself somewhere without knowing where he was or why he was there. He had trouble keeping up with a conversation when there were a lot of people talking. Subsequent investigation revealed that he had Alzheimer's disease.

Ray clearly had deficits in new learning and conscious and contextual memory, indicating a degenerative process in the hippocampus.

EMOTIONS ATTACHED TO THE WRONG MEMORIES – DÉJÀ VU AND JAMAIS VU

There are times when people feel that a place is familiar when they have never been there before. They have an emotional conviction that they 'know' the place but this is not based in reality and their intellect tells them otherwise. Often the same people can feel very unfamiliar with a place, when in fact they know that they have been there before. They have a conviction that it is unfamiliar. These disorders of experiential conviction are typical of hippocampal dysfunction. They represent a failure to have the memory linked to the feelings of familiarity. They are common in epilepsy involving the hippocampus and dementia with hippocampal involvement.

Technical corner

There are many forms of memory, including those mentioned above, to which the hippocampus is integral. Each has a different 'life span'. Memory based in the frontal lobes – working (conscious and short-lived) memory – is the least hardy, as if 'written in sand'. Memory in the hippo-campus (contextual and conscious) is harder to eradicate, as if 'etched in wood'. Basal ganglia memory (unconscious procedural or movement), e.g. riding a bike, is 'woven into the fabric of our daily activities'. Amygdala memory (emotional) is indelible, as if 'chiselled in granite'.

Sage Seahorse in summary

Sage Seahorse lives on Lilly Listentale's estate (temporal lobe) next to his love and companion, Annie Almond (amygdala). He is a calm and wise person, with a remarkable memory for time, place and context, well suited for his position as Head of the Historical Society. He is good friends with Felicity Feelall (thalamus) and Al Zheimer (nucleus of Meynert) and keeps in close touch with the town leadership, especially giving advice, based on his knowledge, to Fredrick Foresight (frontal lobes). When unwell he becomes confused and disoriented, and some-times uncharacteristically emotional.

References

McGuire, E., Frackowiak, R. and Frith, C. (1997) 'Recalling routes around London: activation of the hippocampus in taxi drivers.' *Journal of Neuroscience 17*, 7103–7110.

Further reading

Brumback, R.A. and Leech, R.W. (1996) 'Memories of a seahorse.' *Journal of Child Neurology 11*, 263–264.
O'Keefe, J. and Nadel, L. (2007) 'The hippocampus as a cognitive map.' See www.cognitivemap.net (viewed 14 December 2007).

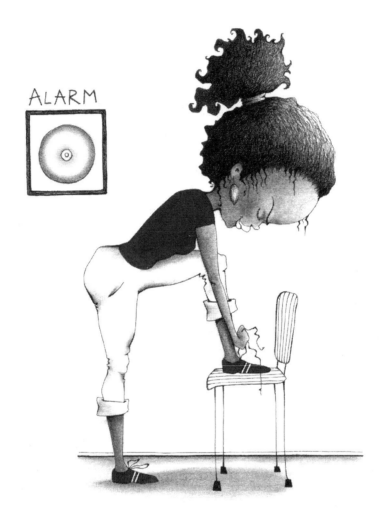

Chapter 13

Annie Almond: the Amygdala

Meet Annie Almond

Annie Almond lives in Midtown next to the very sophisticated Sage Seahorse (hippocampus). Their homes are at the foot of the craggy, white Butterfly Cliffs (Wings of the Spheroid) that mark the boundary between Uptown and Midtown Cephalton. Like Sage, Annie has a remarkably good memory, but hers is for feelings. She feels things 'truly, madly, deeply', without always having time to process why she feels the way she does or having the words to express her powerful passions. Annie judges people and situations quickly, and mostly quite accurately, especially because of her enormous experience.

Annie listens to everything her friend Felicity Feelall (thalamus) says to her. She relays immediately to Annie the feel of what is happening outside Cephalton as she receives it from her many patients in her Polysensory Clinic. Annie listens with a view to registering any potential threats to Cephalton and the Shire beyond.

Uma Underbride (hypothalamus) and her partner, Horace Hormone (pituitary), are Annie's best and most loyal followers. Uma and Horace try to read Annie very closely and respond to how she is feeling. If Annie is upset, Uma moves into action immediately and gets her friend, Rosie Reaction (autonomic nervous system), to mobilise the whole town. Uma will do what Annie wants without question. Annie's other friends,

Fredrick Foresight (frontal lobes), Rochelle Ringbond (cingulate gyrus), Brenda Bridgehead (insula), Priscilla Prizeman (nucleus accumbens) and Sage (hippocampus), all try to be helpful to her and stop her from over-reacting before they have had time to check out what she is worried about. The Downtown Dream Team (reticular formation) has a complicated relationship with Annie. Both Dr Ernie Enkephalin (periaqueductal grey matter) and Tony Turnon (locus coeruleus) are very attached to Annie and respond to her concerns whenever they can.

Sage stays close to Annie, no matter what, knowing that at times she can over-react. When she is under pressure or feeling low, she is prone to thoughts and images of past times of danger and threat crashing into her mind, unable to suppress or forget the pain and traumas of long gone crises. Sometimes at night, she wakes up screaming and in a state of panic, with heart pounding and fear in every part of her body, but unable to recall what the panic was about. When she is very unwell she may react when there is no threat at all, just because of some minor reminder of a past trauma. At these times, she may fail to notice a very real danger and every one in Cephalton is caught unawares. When things are at their worst, she refuses to eat and withdraws from everyone. She even puts all thoughts of her close relationship with Sage to one side and becomes excessively preoccupied with the threat at hand.

The amygdala explained

Location and structure

The amygdala is a small piece of tissue (grey matter) found on an each side of the brain, on the inner side of, and within, the temporal lobes, at the anterior end of the hippocampus. It sits 'cheek by jowl' with the insula cortex. The word 'amygdalum' (singular) means 'an almond seed' in Latin and it was so named because early anatomists thought these pieces of tissue looked like almond seeds. 'Amygdala' (plural) is used by convention even when referring to a single amygdalum.

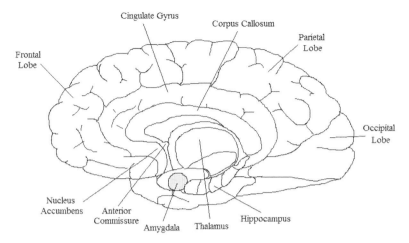

Figure 13.1. Medial view (inner surface) of the right side of the brain showing the amygdala shaded in grey. Each of the main visible lobes of the brain is labelled.

Connections

The amygdala has three main sets of connections:

1. *The cortex.* The amygdala has strong connections with cortical structures, including the frontal lobes, cingulate gyrus, the insula and the somatosensory cortex.

2. *The limbic system.* As part of the emotional brain (limbic system) the amygdala has connections with structures within this system, including the nucleus accumbens, the hippocampus and the hypothalamus.

3. *The brain stem.* The amygdala has strong and diffuse connections with the structures, including components of the reticular formation (Downtown Dream Team), such as the periaqueductal grey matter (Dr Ernie Enkephalin) and the locus coeruleus (Tony Turnon).

Almost all of the amygdala's connections are two-way, but the strength of the output from the amygdala and the remainder of the 'emotional' brain (limbic system) to the 'thinking' brain is far greater than vice versa. Emotions are not easy to control by thought alone because there are

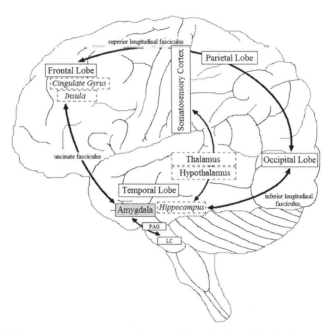

Figure 13.2. Lateral view (outer surface) of the left side of the brain showing a schematic representation of the main connections of the amygdala, with three key functional areas of the brain, including cortical structures, limbic structures and structures in the brain stem. PAG = periaqueductual grey matter; LC = locus coeruleus.

approximately ten times more connections going from the amygdala and the limbic system up to the cognitive centres of the cortex than in reverse. So, for example, the connections between the amygdala and the hippocampus, though travelling in both directions, are very much in favour of the amygdala influencing the hippocampus, rather than the hippocampus affecting the amygdala. Thus conscious experience and memory may be dominated by emotions such as fear and anger. In summary, feelings can overwhelm the more rational thought processes.

Functions

The primary functions of the amygdala are:

* Threat detection.

- Initiating the stress response.

- Implicit emotional learning.

- Multisensory integration of sensory perceptions

THREAT DETECTION

The amygdala can process incoming sensory information in an emergency faster than the conscious reflective capacity of the brain. The smell of fire, a loud unexpected noise, a shadow in the dark, the bitter taste of an acid or alkali or a slither against the skin may all evoke threat detection responses. Frontal lobe processing is relatively slow by comparison with the amygdala. However, the high-order, fine-grained analysis offered by the frontal lobes, together with in-depth problem-solving, complements the rapid and automatic response of the amygdala. The frontal lobes, the hippocampus and the insula provide some inhibition of impulsive responses and an over-ride system to modulate responses in the light of 'the facts' in the outside world.

INITIATING THE STRESS RESPONSE

Figure 13.3 illustrates the pathway involved in the response to stress. Having received 'threatening' sensory information from the thalamus, the amygdala sends information to the hypothalamus, which in turn activates the autonomic nervous system, leading to 'flight or fight or fright' and 'shut down' responses. It also releases hormones, which set off a longer-term stress response (corticotropin releasing hormone, CRH, which regulates cortisol release).

IMPLICIT EMOTIONAL (SINGLE TRIAL) LEARNING

Through its connections to the frontal lobes, the amygdala is intimately connected with learning, especially longer-term, and is resistant to forgetting. It is responsible for 'once only' or 'single trial learning' as opposed to so many other forms of memory that require repetition and rehearsal to prevent forgetting. For example, if a person or object

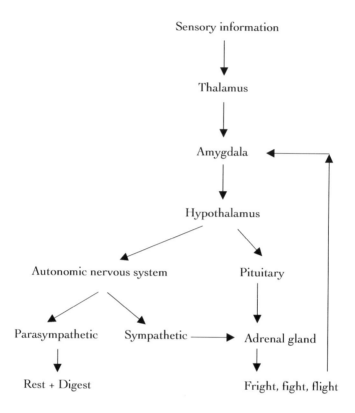

Figure 13.3. The pathway of the stress response

is associated (coincidentally or otherwise) with a traumatic episode, then encountering that person or object at a later time, however un-threatening they might be in reality, will invoke a stress response, without there necessarily being any awareness as to why. This learning and its resultant memories are relatively indelible, as if 'chiselled in granite' (see Technical corner in Chapter 12).

MULTISENSORY INTEGRATION

The amygdala is one of the key zones where different sensations converge. Having made a 'quick and dirty' risk assessment and, if neces-sary, initiated the stress response, the amygdala relays information to the hippocampus and to the frontal lobes, where jointly a more detailed and informed analysis of the information is conducted.

When things go wrong

A number of different disorders are associated with amygdala dysfunction and are believed to arise from either increased or decreased amygdala sensitivity and activity.

DISORDERS ASSOCIATED WITH AMYGDALA OVERSENSITIVITY AND OVERACTIVITY

1. *Night terrors.* These are thought to involve bursts of amygdala activity, with sympathetic nervous system arousal, in stage three or four of orthodox sleep.

2. *Panic attacks.* These are believed to be the result of a similar process to that of night terrors, and are likely to be related to the strength of the amygdala's activity. It is almost impossible to ignore the cascade of responses initiated by the amygdala, and played out by the hypothalamus, pituitary and autonomic nervous systems.

3. *Post-traumatic stress disorder (PTSD).* This is thought to be due to oversensitivity and overactivity of the amygdala. It often results from the experience of a severe emotional and/or physical trauma from which there is no immediate escape, leading to a sense of helplessness. The more emotionally charged the event, the more aroused is the amygdala and the more indelible is the emotional memory.

Sandy, aged 15, who has a long history of physical abuse by her mother, as well as an experience of sexual assault by a stranger, suffers from post-traumatic stress disorder (PTSD). She frequently experiences flashbacks of both her assault and repetitive abuse. She becomes very distressed when things are said or done that remind her of either trauma. When these cues for her memories occur she begins to have physical symptoms of anxiety and starts to relive her trauma. It is almost impossible for her to put these thoughts from her mind.

DISORDERS ASSOCIATED WITH AMYGDALA UNDERSENSITIVITY
AND UNDERACTIVITY

The most common disorder is that of antisocial personality disorder (commonly referred as psychopathy). Such people display emotional coldness, bullying, deceit, lack of remorse and enjoyment in risk-taking. Brain scans reveal underactivity of the amygdala when the subject is exposed to threatening stimuli or is exposed to another person's distress.

The classic amygdala case: Dr Edouard Claparede's patient

A classic case, where emotional memory of threat is intact although conscious memory is impaired, is discussed in a book, *The Emotional Brain* (1998), by Joseph LeDoux, considered the world's leading authority on the amygdala.

Dr Edouard Claparede was a French physician who in 1911 described a female patient with brain damage of such severity that she was unable to create new memories. For example, each time Claparede walked into the room to see her, he would have to reintroduce himself as she had no memory of ever meeting him before. Her memory loss for him even occurred when he had to leave the room for a few minutes during the same session.

Claparede decided to test his patient's memory in another way. Once when he walked into the room to see her and reintroduce himself, he held out his hand to greet her as per usual. However, this time he placed a tack in the palm of his hand and when she went to shake his hand, the tack pricked her and she quickly pulled away her hands. The next time Claperede saw her he once again introduced himself and again she did not remember him. However, this time she refused to shake his outstretched hand. Claperede's patient could not inform him why she did not wish to shake his hand but just refused to do so. Therefore, while Claperede's patient had no conscious memory of when she had been pricked by the tack in his hand, she did have a subconscious memory that shaking his hand was dangerous and that she must not do so in future (even though consciously she could never remember him).

Her brain damage prevented her from having conscious (declarative) memories (hippocampus), although she was still able to have subconscious and emotional (implicit) memories (amygdala). This case indicates the development of an emotional memory, which can be laid down in a single episode of learning. Such memories, formed via the amygdala, are often the most resilient.

Annie Almond in summary

Annie, living in Midtown, is well placed to have contact with many of the key members of the community. She is vital, dynamic and passionate, and is intimately involved with Sage Seahorse (hippocampus). Close friends include Fredrick Foresight (frontal lobes), Rochelle Ringbond (cingulate gyrus), Brenda Bridgehead (insula), Priscilla Prizeman (nucleus accumbens), Dr Ernie Enkephalin (periaqueductal grey matter) and Tony Turnon (locus coeruleus). Her main role is to keep an eye open for danger. She is alert to any suggestion of threat, initiating an appropriate response, which is in part based upon her great store of memories of feelings.

If she is unwell she tends to either over- or under-react. When overreacting she becomes extremely anxious and even panic-stricken. When under-reacting she becomes unfeeling, un-empathic and even at times antisocial.

Reference

LeDoux, J. (1998) *The Emotional Brain: The Mysterious Underpinnings of Emotional Life.* New York, NY: Phoenix.

Further reading

Aggleton, J.P. (1992) *The Amygdala: Neurobiological Aspects of Emotion, Memory, and Mental Dysfunction.* Brisbane: Wiley-Liss.
Brizendine, L. (2006) *The Female Brain.* New York, NY: Broadway Books.

Chapter 14

Priscilla Prizeman and Olivia Orgasmia: the Nucleus Accumbens and Septal Nuclei

Meet Priscilla Prizeman and Olivia Orgasmia

Priscilla lives in Midtown Cephalton on the edge of the very beautiful, but awesomely craggy, butterfly cliffs (sphenoid bone), surrounded by the huge compound owned by Fredrick Foresight (frontal lobes) and Rochelle Ringbond (cingulate gyrus). Priscilla's home overlooks one of the most beautiful canyons in Cephalton, affectionately referred to as Turkish Saddle Canyon (sella turcica) because it resembles the high front and back of the saddles used by the Turks in ancient times. Her home is so elevated, she has supplies brought up from Midtown from her own business on Lake Undercover (ventral tegmentum). She gets supplies not only for herself but for much of Uptown Cephalton.

Priscilla is a shrewd business woman and is in partnership with Corrie O'Graphie (basal ganglia) and Annie Almond (amygdala). She also has her own advertising business and casino. There is no doubt she is one of the most powerful women in Cephalton, especially because of the very strong influence she has over Fredrick Foresight (frontal lobes). But it is not only Fredrick she influences. She drives the whole Uptown agenda while keeping her feet very much on the ground with the Midtown movers and mood. She has a good working relationship with Al Zheimer (nucleus of Meynert) and Sage Seahorse (hippocampus). She is the 'behind the scenes' person who is always sensitive to what others have said. If they give her good feedback she is over the moon and makes them feel that way too, without saying a word.

Priscilla has always been quite a party girl, whether mixing with 'the movers and shakers' in town, or with some of the more earthy 'let's get down to it' action people. She is often to be found in search of fun and she is driven to seek the rewards of life. Like everyone in Cephalton, she has her weaknesses. She has a reputation for getting hooked on a particular activity and becoming completely taken over by it. She has tremendous drive and when it is harnessed for good she is hard to beat. But, in the past, she has found it hard to resist the world of drugs (cocaine, amphetamines and heroin as well as marijuana, alcohol and cigarettes), sex, gambling and chocolate. When she is on an even keel, the things that switch her on are exercise and being told that she looks great. When she gets the rewards that she wants in life she has so much to give but, when she doesn't, the demons of her former life seem close at hand. An orgy of self-destructive, addictive behaviour, which is entirely heedless of her best friends' advice and entreaties, can take over every part of her life. At the extreme she becomes confused, chaotic and thought-disordered with hallucinations and delusions.

Priscilla lets out some of her property to the glamorous Olivia Orgasmia (septal nuclei), one of the most colourful of Cephalton's characters. She lives in a small and beautiful crescent-shaped building in the grounds of Priscilla's home. Olivia is a connoisseur of intense and ecstatic pleasure, possibly her raison d'être. This is almost exclusively sexually focused and she has been known to take many lovers. Rumour has it that she is not averse to sexual experimentation. Indeed, there is much speculation about the relationship between Olivia and Priscilla for they are obviously close and have much in common. Olivia's soirees are very exclusive and Priscilla is almost always invited. But what then happens between them remains one of Cephalton's most closely guarded secrets.

When Olivia is unwell she becomes frustrated and irritable, unable to achieve the satisfaction she craves. This is readily communicated to Priscilla and it is not long before everyone knows that all is not well and the whole community becomes frustrated. Some of the further reaches of the Shire are particularly sensitive to Olivia's failure with a lowering of spirits and a drying up of enthusiasm. When her own frustration is too much to bear she tends to experience intense rages and sometimes complete loss of control.

The nucleus accumbens explained

The nucleus accumbens is sometimes listed with the basal ganglia and sometimes with the limbic system. This is because it connects the systems involved with movement with those systems involved with mood. Sometimes the nucleus accumbens is given a standing all of its own as the 'reward circuitry' of the brain. This serves to remind us that each of these systems has an intimate relationship with the memory systems of the brain and that reward and reinforcement are part of the more general functions of learning and memory.

Location and structure

The nucleus accumbens is a subcortical structure – a small piece of tissue that lies just below and behind the frontal lobes, at the front end of the corpus callosum. It is called accumbens because it leans up against the septal nuclei (just as recumbent means to 'lie back' so accumbens means to 'lie toward'). It is also close to the caudate nuclei and the basal nucleus of Meynert and just in front of the sella turcica in which the hypothalamus and pituitary are found.

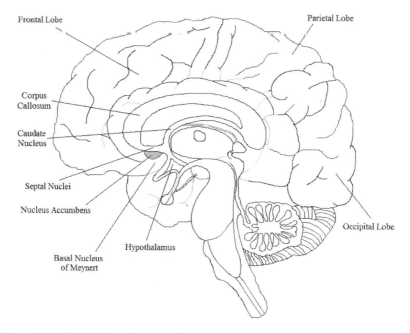

Frontal Lobe

Parietal Lobe

Corpus
Callosum

Caudate
Nucleus

Septal Nuclei

Nucleus Accumbens

Occipital Lobe

Hypothalamus

Basal Nucleus
of Meynert

Figure 14.1. Medial view (inner surface) of the right side of the brain showing the nucleus accumbens shaded in grey. Each of the visible main lobes of the brain is labelled.

Connections

As the nucleus accumbens is one of the brain's main centres for the production and storage of dopamine, it is intimately connected with several brain regions involving this neurotransmitter. The brain has several pathways for dopamine distribution (see Technical corner, p.151) and the nucleus accumbens is connected to all of them in some way. These connecting pathways include the following:

MENTAL ACTIVITY – MEMORY PATHWAYS

This pathway (mesocortical dopamine pathway) connects the nucleus accumbens to the brain regions involved in concentration, thinking and working memory such as the cingulate gyrus (Rochelle Ringbond), the frontal lobes (Fredrick Foresight) and the nucleus of Meynert (Al Zheimer).

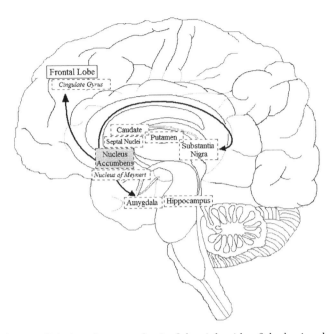

Figure 14.2. Medial view (inner surface) of the right side of the brain, showing a schematic representation of the main connections of the nucleus accumbens. Note the intimate relationship between the nucleus accumbens (reward system), the septal nuclei (intense emotional experience) and the basal ganglia (movement system).

MOOD – MEMORY PATHWAYS

The nucleus accumbens is connected with those brain regions responsible for mood and memory (mesolimbic dopamine pathways), especially the amygdala (Annie Almond) and the hippocampus (Sage Seahorse – declarative or conscious experiential memory).

MOVEMENT – MEMORY PATHWAYS

The nucleus accumbens has strong connections to the brain regions responsible for movement such as the caudate nucleus, the putamen and the substantia nigra (nigrostriatal dopamine pathway). In some places the caudate and the nucleus accumbens merge into one another. These structures are collectively known as the basal ganglia (Corrie O'Graphie). The basal ganglia underlie skill-based procedural memory.

Functions

There are two main functions of the nucleus accumbens which are intimately connected with one another and both rely on memory:

Reward and reinforcement

- Links rewards of primary needs such as food, drink, sex and nurture to other situations (conditioned stimuli or cues) via various forms of memory

- Prediction of likely reward – hopefulness (non-verbal)

- Identifying when expected rewards do not come (non-verbal disappointment)

Motivation and drive

- Linking movement, mood, motivation and memory to goal-directed thinking

REWARD AND REINFORCEMENT

The nucleus accumbens rewards and reinforces behaviours essential for survival by linking emotion and memory. The release of dopamine in this area is responsible for making sure that behaviours are reinforced, often by being consciously pleasurable. The nucleus accumbens rewards the primary drives such as food, drink, sex and nurture. The nucleus accumbens also has an anticipatory role in relation to reward, predicting the likelihood that something will be rewarding (creating hopes and expectations at a very fundamental, non-verbal level) and identifying when reward has not occurred (non-verbal basis of disappointment).

The nucleus accumbens deals not only with primary drives but all those matters that are conditioned to be associated with them in an individual's life. This means that places and associations (cues) with these primary rewards come to be rewarded, as well as being part of memory.

For example, advertising works on the nucleus accumbens to encourage people to buy the product being advertised. Most advertising uses primary drive associations such as food, drink, sex and nurture to link to the product. Another example is the way in which many people associate the time after a meal with friends, with drinking and smoking. Video games and music also work their powerful effect through the reward circuitry of the nucleus accumbens.

This does not mean that the nucleus accumbens *always* creates pleasure. It functions to make us *want*, even if we don't *like*. It is possible for a person to come to hate his or her needs, obsessions, addictions or compulsions but to be unable to stop seeking fulfilment. Reward is happening mainly at a chemical level and only secondarily at a conscious level. Reinforcement is a description of the largely unconscious promotion of behaviour, not feelings. Sometimes the reward is associated with good feeling, but it is not always so. Wanting, yearning, hoping and craving are different to enjoying, liking and feeling good.

MOTIVATION AND DRIVE

The nucleus accumbens produces motivation and drive by linking the emotional systems (limbic system) to the movement systems (basal ganglia). Both of these systems are heavily implicated in memory. It links the movement systems (action), the memory systems (past experience) and the emotional systems (feelings) to produce motivation within the cognitive systems (thinking). That is, motivation represents motor action, which is energised by emotion, informed by past experience and guided by cognitive goals. The nucleus accumbens plays a central role in creating the drives that keep people going and that are disappointed when goals are frustrated.

When things go wrong

The nucleus accumbens, when disordered, can give rise to the rewarding and reinforcement of maladaptive behaviours and alterations in motivation and drive.

THE REWARDING OF MALADAPTIVE BEHAVIOURS – ADDICTION

Many drugs of addiction work on the nucleus accumbens and reinforce behaviour associated with the drugs and the setting in which they are taken. Drugs that cause an increase in dopamine can overstimulate the nucleus accumbens, giving pleasure, rewarding drug use and reinforcing harmful behaviour. Almost all major drugs of abuse work directly or indirectly with the dopamine system in the nucleus accumbens and other areas.

Drugs that increase dopamine activity directly include amphetamines, cocaine and nicotine, while drugs that have an indirect effect include heroin, alcohol and marijuana. Reasoning does not have much impact on these behaviours and everything is assessed in terms of whether it satisfies the craving.

Cocaine blocks the re-uptake of dopamine and noradrenalin by neurons that synapse in the nucleus accumbens. Amphetamines and methamphetamine increase the release of dopamine and noradrenalin from neurons that synapse in the nucleus accumbens. The reinforcing properties of psychostimulant drugs have been found to be proportional to their ability to increase the action of dopamine in the nucleus accumbens.

> Jack, 35, has a chronic addiction to amphetamines. He grew up in an abusive, praise-deprived home and his mother was depressed for most of his early life. He used to smoke a lot of cannabis and drink alcohol heavily in his early teenage years. Jack still finds that he readily becomes addicted to any illicit drug that he takes. He experiences severe withdrawal and urges when he does not have access to any alcohol or drugs and is always trying to find ways to obtain his next drug 'hit'. Sometimes Jack becomes so desperate he assaults others and steals from them. He has nothing else in his life as rewarding as taking drugs.

Jack's history of maternal depression and paternal violence suggests that he may have been deprived, as a baby and young child, of rewarding experiences and therefore the normal reasons for dopamine activity in the nucleus accumbens. Many people who abuse illicit drugs come from dysfunctional families, have experienced early abuse, neglect and deprivation and often have lower dopamine activity. This may lead to a compensatory increase in use of dopamine through other means such as illicit drug-taking.

SCHIZOPHRENIA

Positive symptoms of schizophrenia, such as disordered thinking, delusions, hallucinations and bizarre or socially inappropriate behaviour, appear to be related to excessive activity of dopamine neurons in the nucleus accumbens or other areas of the limbic system (mesolimbic pathways). Drugs that block dopamine transmission (dopamine antagonists) help treat these positive symptoms. Negative symptoms of schizophrenia, such as loss of imaginative thought, loss of emotional and social responsiveness and lack of motivation are thought to be due to underactivity of dopaminergic systems in the nucleus accumbens and the frontal lobes.

Technical corner

The nucleus accumbens is the basic forebrain nucleus for the neurotransmitter dopamine. Dopamine is a key chemical communicator in the brain. It is one of the activating chemicals like its relatives, adrenaline and noradrenaline. All three are called catecholamines and the precursors to dopamine are found in proteins in our diet.

The nucleus accumbens links the basal ganglia and the limbic system. The nucleus accumbens, the nearby ventral tegmentum (Lake Undercover) and the substantia nigra are the main centres for the production and storage of dopamine to supply the frontal lobes in front and above, and the basal ganglia behind and below (see Table 14.2). Its main functions consist of reward conditioning, memory and drive to meet perceived needs. Addiction, as a phenomenon, is linked to reward conditioning, which is in turn linked to pulsatile secretion of dopamine from the nucleus accumbens.

Table 14.2. The nucleus accumbens and the dopamine pathways

1. Mesocortical pathway – disruption of this pathway by too little dopamine activity leads to negative symptoms of schizophrenia.

2. Mesolimbic pathways – disruption of this pathway with overactivity of dopamine neurons produces the positive symptoms of schizophrenia.

3. Nigrostriatal pathways – disruption of this pathway by too little dopamine produces the side-effects of the older style antipsychotic medications. Muscle stiffness in jaw muscles, eye movement muscles and the large muscles of the neck and back, Parkinsonian symptoms and tardive dyskinesia (a serious, late onset movement disorder).

4. Tuberoinfundibular pathways – disruption of this pathway by too little dopamine gives rise to increased secretion of prolactin and milk produced from the breasts of some women taking antipsychotic medications (galactorrhoea) and decreased sexual libido in men.

The septal nuclei explained

Location

The septal nuclei are midline structures immediately next to the nucleus accumbens at the lower front end of the corpus callosum.

Connections

The septal nuclei have reciprocal connections with the nucleus accumbens (reward circuitry) and limbic system structures (emotional circuitry), including the cingulate gyrus, hippocampus, amygdala and hypothalamus.

Functions

The functions of the septal nuclei are far from clear but appear to include associations with (a) sexual consummation and reward – orgasm is linked to activation of the septal nuclei and is in turn a powerfully reinforced experience, presumably at least in part due to its close connection with the nucleus accumbens; and (b) the expression of rage – the mechanism is not understood but may be associated with inhibition of the amygdala, i.e. the septal nuclei may normally put a brake on the amygdala.

When things go wrong

Problems with the septal nuclei result in difficulties with orgasm and rage. For example, tumours in the septal nuclei can lead to outbursts of rage (so called septal rage).

Priscilla Prizeman and Olivia Orgasmia in summary

Priscilla (nucleus accumbens) is an important part of the motivational life of Cephalton, joining together the very different characters, Fredrick Foresight and Rochelle Ringbond (mental activity), Annie Almond and Sage Seahorse (mood and memory) and Corrie O'Graphy (movement) in a powerful concerted team. She gives much pleasure and lots of rewards (dopamine). But the rewards have risks if she is overcome by her demons and all her strengths become self-destructive, with addictions, gambling, and exploitation of her most basic needs. When she is over-excited she can become acutely psychotic or addicted to drugs, gambling and a life of seeking instant reward. When she is under-stimulated she is apathetic, unresponsive and lacking the initiative and drive required to cope with everyday life.

Olivia Orgasmia (septal nuclei), Priscilla's close friend and neighbour, has sexual satisfaction as her raison d'être. When thwarted she can experience intense rages and her frustration has a demoralising effect on Cephalton and the Shire.

Further reading

Gazzaniga, M.S., Ivry, R.B. and Mangun, G.R. (2002) *Cognitive Neuroscience: The Biology of the Mind.* New York, NY: Norton.

Kalat, J.W. (2003) *Biological Psychology* (8th edition). South Melbourne: Thomson Wadsworth.

Chapter 15

Corrie O'Graphie: the Basal Ganglia

Meet Corrie O'Graphie

Corrie, a wonderfully talented dancer, lives on the border of Uptown and Midtown, immediately next to Felicity Feelall's (thalamus) island home, mixing with both social groups with apparent ease. Truth be told, though, she finds the Midtown group easier to relate to. She is an essential member of daily life in Cephalton, although to look at her you would never guess what a critical role she plays. She does not have a high public profile in the politics of town life and keeps her visibility to a minimum. She never makes a fuss about things. It is only with time and an in-depth knowledge of Cephalton that it becomes apparent that nothing gets done without her.

When Corrie walks down the street she seems to glide with astounding poise, posture and subtlety of movement. These reflect the years of dance training that have shaped every fibre of her being and stamped the complex sequences of a thousand choreographic routines into even the most spontaneous of her movements. Somehow that poise makes everyone else attempt to be a little more stylish in the way they do things. All eyes turn to her quite automatically and everyone is guided by the way she moves.

Having been around for a long time, Corrie knows how to get things done and keeps activities in the town from stalling. She has a plan, procedure, routine and protocol for every occasion so that everything runs smoothly without people having to think about it and without them being aware of her constant input. When there is a decision in the town to change the way things are done, initially everyone works hard at following the new approach. Fredrick Foresight (frontal cortex) and Dudley Doit (motor cortex) lead the change whilst Corrie and Frank Finesse (cerebellum), her best friend, as well as her dance partner, help the whole town in the transition. But, as time goes by, it is Corrie who keeps working on making the changes permanent. She is the corporate memory for how things are to be done.

Corrie is very attuned to others. She listens especially to her other neighbours, Annie Almond (amygdala), who tells her how people are feeling, and Priscilla Prizeman (nucleus accumbens), who is able to tell her that her efforts are worthwhile. She then sends messages via her nearest neighbour Felicity Feelall (thalamus) to Fredrick and Dudley who always take note.

Corrie and Frank are one of the great partnerships in Cephalton. How did such a small town end up with two of the finest dancers the world has ever seen? That is still a mystery. They are both older now but they are still a great team and they make the rest of the town a team too. At the Annual Ball they regularly win the trophy for grace and elegance on the ballroom floor. Together they set the tone for each event. She never makes a speech herself but every public speech is monitored by Frank and Corrie for clarity, tone and timing.

When Corrie becomes unwell she loses the extraordinary flair and panache of her beautiful, flowing movements. Sometimes she actually slows down and shakes, walking like a very old woman with a shuffle. At other times, she jerks and twists suddenly, without any real control over her movements. When she is at her very worst, she finds it hard to get out of bed and get going. She may become depressed and even immobile. She loses her drive and concentration. Strangely, or perhaps mercifully, at these times she is not fully aware of the extraordinary changes that have taken place in her appearance and demeanour.

This illness runs in her family and is all the more tragic because of the contrast between when Corrie is ill and when she is well. The whole town feels for her. Her movements and the town's mood seem somehow to move in synchrony with one another. It seems especially cruel when she is usually so very dignified and the contortions of her illness may make others pity her. Such effects on her friends and neighbours show how vital she is to the community and are, in a strange way, a tribute to her.

The basal ganglia explained

Location and structure

The basal ganglia are a cluster of knots of grey matter (nuclei) lying deep beneath the outer surface of the brain and for this reason are called subcortical structures (i.e. under the cortex). They are situated towards the base of the front of the brain and along both sides of the thalamus.

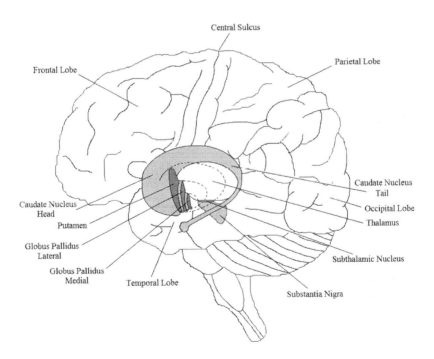

Figure 15.1. Lateral view (outer surface) of the left side of the brain showing the basal ganglia, in transparency, shaded in grey. Each of the visible main lobes of the brain is labelled.

Experts often argue as to what parts of the brain are, or are not, in the basal ganglia. However, the general consensus is that the basal ganglia include:

1. *The putamen* – like most of these nuclei, there is one putamen on each side of the brain. The ancient word from which putamen is derived means 'pruned' or cut away from the nucleus next to it, the caudate.

2. *The caudate nuclei* – so called because it has a tail. Together, the putamen and the caudate have a striped appearance. The ancient word for 'striped' was striatum, and so some refer to these two knots of grey matter as 'the striatum'. The tail of the caudate lies behind the amygdala and the head lies underneath the corpus callosum, bulging into the wall of the third ventricle.

3. *The globus pallidus* – so called because of its pale appearance, due to some white matter fibres running through it. It is adjacent to and beneath the striatum, just in front of the nucleus accumbens. It is a round, pale, ball-like part of the brain, about the size of a small marble.

4. *The substantia nigra* – so called because of its black appearance due to melanin content. This is the deepest part of the basal ganglia and the closest to the midline. It lies beneath the thalamus and on the medial aspect of the globus pallidus.

Connections

The basal ganglia have three main sets of connections that reflect their functions:

1. *Motor connections.* The cortex sends messages via the putamen to the rest of the body about where the body is in space (somatosensory cortex), preparatory signals that movements are about to happen (premotor cortex) and the actual signals initiating movement (primary motor cortex). All of these

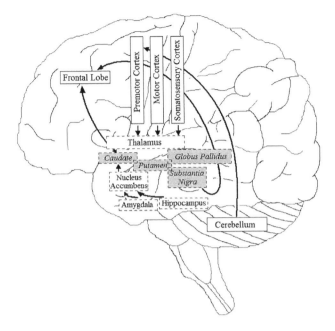

Figure 15.2. Lateral view (outer surface) of the left side of the brain showing a schematic representation of the main connections of the basal ganglia. Note the intimate connections between the emotional brain (amygdala and hippocampus) and the basal ganglia (movement system).

messages relay in the thalamus together with messages from the other movement-regulating centre, the cerebellum, so that movement and muscle tone can be altered from moment to moment. The caudate nucleus sends signals to the centres in the frontal lobes regulating eye movement in order to ensure high-level coordination of eye movement with other bodily activities.

2. *Memory, emotional and motivational connections.* The temporal lobes (listening and comprehension), hippocampi (contextual memory) and amygdala (threat detection) all send information via the nucleus accumbens (motivation and possible reward) to the striatum in order to link emotions with motivation, so that both can be linked to movement to produce action.

3. *Sensory connections.* There is a constant conversation between the thalamus and the basal ganglia. The motor cortex and the cerebellum also communicate with the thalamus. This enables all movements to be integrated with the latest incoming information in the planning of movement to incorporate which movement patterns and sequences will be needed.

The pathways travelling out of the basal ganglia and making connections in these different parts of the brain can be remembered by thinking of 'the black and the white'. The two output pathways are from the substantia nigra (black) and the globus pallidus (white).

Functions

The basal ganglia have three main functions:

* Implementing movement

* Procedural memory

* Regulating muscle tone

IMPLEMENTING MOVEMENT

The basal ganglia are the parts of the brain which, when instructed by the motor cortex, enable the body to carry out a wide range of movements, without having to allocate conscious thought to the process. These movements may be simple, such as walking, or more complex, such as riding a bike, and are enabled through detailed preplanned sequences, memory for which is the second function of the basal ganglia (see below).

Within the basal ganglia there are two main pathways for processing movement information. The direct (activating) pathway goes straight to the outflow pathways and gives the 'go ahead' for the movement with some added information to get the movement right. The indirect (inhibitory) pathway involves extra time for processing and allows for inhibition of movement.

PROCEDURAL MEMORY

The basal ganglia provide the deep, unspoken memory called procedural memory which makes it possible to do things years later that may have been consciously 'forgotten' for so long. Some people are surprised to find that although they may not have done so for a long time, they can still ski, ride a bike, drive a car or play a piano. They contain an archive of routines, which can be accessed and sequenced to do tasks that may require many complex movements.

This 'habit learning' can be exemplified by considering what happens when driving a car. The sequences involved when first learning to drive seem awkward and need to be consciously thought about and practised repeatedly. The frontal lobes and the cerebellum make greater contributions at first while the tasks are still new or novel. Later they become much smoother and less effortful until 'practice makes perfect' – procedural memory.

REGULATING MUSCLE TONE

The balance between the direct and indirect pathways creates the level of activity and muscle tone for any movement which does not enter conscious thought. This system of regulating the muscle tone is sometimes referred to as the extrapyramidal system because it was thought to lie alongside, but outside of, the general motor pathways, which were called the pyramidal pathways. It is now recognised that the entire system is regulated within the basal ganglia.

When things go wrong

The basal ganglia are associated with a number of relatively common disorders that are usually referred to as movement disorders. However, they are also associated with some major neuropsychiatric presentations. The disorders may reflect:

1. Overactivity of the basal ganglia

2. Underactivity of the basal ganglia

3. Mixture of both overactivity under-activity

CONDITIONS REFLECTING OVERACTIVITY OF THE BASAL GANGLIA
Tourette's syndrome

Tourette's syndrome, named after the nineteenth-century physician, George Gilles de la Tourette, is a movement disorder characterised by unusual movements affecting the face, neck, vocal cords and limbs. The abnormal movements are often accompanied by unusual noises or the utterance of obscenities (coprolalia). It is commonly associated with obsessive compulsive disorder and attention deficit. Most sufferers possess normal or above normal intelligence and are aware of their uncontrollable movements and verbal utterances.

> Adrian, ten years old, suffers from Tourette's syndrome. Since he was around four years old he has had twitches of his face and body. As he began to speak and later went to school he began yelling out swear words unintentionally. At first his teachers thought he was being rude and trying to be funny for his classmates. However, Adrian would become distressed afterwards and apologise. His teacher has now had to explain to his peers and other staff members about his condition to prevent him from being punished. However, Adrian admits that occasionally he will swear out loud at someone when they really annoy him and blame it on his Tourette's. Adrian has found that sometimes he can contain his twitches and swearing for a short while. After he has successfully suppressed them he finds they will intensify for a while.

The exact cause of Tourette's syndrome is unknown. However, it is thought to be related to overactivity of the dopamine system within the basal ganglia. Samuel Johnson and Mozart are examples of famous people with Tourette's syndrome.

Huntington's chorea (also known as Huntington disease)

Huntington's chorea is a hereditary degenerative disease, characterised by involuntary and irregular jerking movements and progressive mental deterioration. Initially there are jerky arm movements and facial twitches. Later stages of the disease include tremors, writhing movements, depression, memory impairment, hallucinations and delusions.

The basal ganglia are highly affected in Huntington's chorea with loss of nerve cells in the caudate nuclei and putamen. It is believed to be caused by a gene defect on chromosome four. It is uncommon for a sufferer to show symptoms prior to age 30 although there are cases beginning in childhood. No treatment is currently available for the dementia component, but the movement and mood components have been treated with mixed results. In the early stages of Huntington's chorea, the indirect (inhibitory) pathway is more affected than the direct (activating) pathway. This leads to a loss of brakes on movement and un-dampened accelerators, i.e. movement increases. As the illness progresses the direct (activating) pathway also deteriorates and the picture begins to resemble Parkinson's disease.

> Jane is a 29-year-old doctor whose mother has Huntington's chorea and whose grandmother recently died from it. Jane had assisted with her grandmother's care and was now helping her mother by feeding and bathing her and looking after her during the night. Jane is researching Huntington's chorea and knows the latest research very well. She has decided not to have the genetic screening as she is aware of her high risk of inheriting the disease and does not want to know if she has it. Jane had decided not to have children, as she knows they would have a 50 per cent chance of inheriting the disorder if she is a carrier. However, she is now reconsidering this in the light of antenatal testing.

Most people who are at risk of developing Huntington's chorea decide not to have the genetic screening as they worry they will find out they have it and then live in fear of its onset and progress. Relatives of those with Huntington's chorea undergo genetic counselling before deciding to have the tests to determine if they will inherit the disorder.

Woody Guthrie, whom Bob Dylan immortalised in one of his songs, was a famous folk and blues singer who developed Huntington's chorea. His wife began one of the biggest charitable organisations in the world for sufferers.

Obsessive compulsive disorder (OCD)

OCD is linked to dysfunction of the basal ganglia, as indicated by brain scans showing increased activity. People with OCD have repetitive disturbing thoughts and then conduct repetitive actions or rituals in an attempt to prevent the thoughts from coming true. Sufferers from OCD know that these thoughts are illogical and that the preventative efforts are fruitless, but nonetheless feel compelled to keep doing them. The part of the basal ganglia most active in the brain scans of those with OCD is the caudate nucleus and it has been hypothesised that the abnormality involves a circuit connecting the caudate nuclei and the frontal lobes.

The classic basal ganglia case: OCD

Henrik Ibsen, 1828–1906, is second only to Shakespeare as the world's most performed dramatist. Behind his brilliant writing was a neurotic personality tormented by the need for pedantic rituals and absolute punctuality. Every day, having dressed in the most meticulous of ways, at precisely 10.30 a.m. he would put down his pen and walk to the Grand Café in Oslo. There he would insist on sitting at the same table, set in the same way, having the same specially imported German beer, and read his newspapers according to a predetermined system. Any breach of his many daily rituals led him into a state of extreme anxiety and confusion. Should someone be even a few seconds late for an appointment with him he would send them away, even his own barber.

CONDITIONS REFLECTING UNDERACTIVITY OF THE BASAL GANGLIA

Cannabis use

Cannabis contains over 400 chemicals, of which around 60 have direct effects on the brain, tetrahydrocannabinol (THC) being the most potent. THC acts by reducing the firing of neurons in the regions with THC receptor sites, one of which is the basal ganglia. The motor functions usually carried out in this region are consequently impaired.

Jack, 25, was studying law at university. He had been at a party with his friends, celebrating the end of his examinations, where he smoked cannabis. He thought it was safe to drive as he had not been drinking alcohol, but he failed to negotiate a bend, over-steered to avoid a tree, and crashed into an oncoming vehicle. He and several of his friends were killed instantly.

THC inhibits the normal basal ganglia function, and normal movement procedures such as driving are impaired. Many victims of fatal accidents, such as Jack, have been found to have THC in their blood.

Parkinson's disease

Parkinson's disease, named after James Parkinson who first described it in the early nineteenth century in an essay on 'the shaking palsy', is associated with deterioration of the basal ganglia. The disease occurs in around one to two people per thousand and is found equally across genders. The risk of developing Parkinson's disease increases as a person ages and usually has an onset after the age of 50. The features of Parkinson's disease include tremor, lack of facial movement, speech difficulties, stooped posture, shuffling walk, and general slowness of movement. During later stages of the disease, cognitive decline, such as difficulties with memory, reasoning and attention, occurs. Depression and dementia are often part of the process.

The basal ganglia in those with Parkinson's disease have decreased pigmentation and neuronal loss, due predominantly to progressive cell death in the substantia nigra. Most people lose small amounts of these neurons as they age (after age 45 a person may lose one per cent per year). However, those with Parkinson's disease may lose around 20–30 per cent per year. There are decreased levels of the neurotransmitters, dopamine and norepinephrine, and medical treatment is predominantly focused on restoring neurotransmitter balance. L-dopa, although not effective in every case of Parkinson's disease, is the most common pharmacological treatment, as it crosses the blood–brain barrier and enters the neurons that convert it into dopamine.

Famous sufferers of Parkinson's disease include:

Pope John Paul II

The Pope, who was once a very athletic man, started to show signs of Parkinson's disease in the 1990s when his left hand had a significant tremor. The public questioned whether he had the illness but his medical team would not comment. In 2001, when the Pope was 80 years old, one of his doctors informed the media that the Pope did indeed have Parkinson's disease.

Michael J. Fox

Michael J. Fox is a famous and popular American actor who appeared in many TV series and movies in the 1980s and 1990s and won many television awards for his acting and popularity. He was diagnosed with early onset Parkinson's disease in 1991 but did not disclose this to the public until 1998. At that time, Fox was starring in a popular American television show and was showing marked signs of the disease such as a tremor, stiff gait and facial grimaces. Fox used props and judicious use of medication to help disguise these symptoms. However, by 2000 he retired from acting and focused on establishing the Michael. J. Fox Foundation that researches treatments for Parkinson's disease as well as raises the public's awareness of the disorder. Fox has set a goal for the Foundation to find a cure for Parkinson's disease by 2010. He appeared before the US Senate to give evidence about the suffering of those with Parkinson's disease and the need for research funding into its causes.

Muhammad Ali

Muhammad Ali is one of the world's most famous boxers and has been described as one of the greatest athletes of the twentieth century. He was a gold medal Olympian and won many world heavyweight champion-ships. Ali retired from boxing in 1981 and publicly announced his disease in 1984. Ali has displayed the progressive signs of deterioration such as marked tremor, shuffle gait and a stone face. He, like Fox, has become a full-time fundraiser in the fight for a cure for Parkinson's disease.

Corrie O'Graphie in summary

Corrie (basal ganglia) lives on the border of Uptown and Midtown, and despite being essential to the life of Cephalton and a wonderful dancer, tends to keep a low profile. She is well organised and quietly ensures that everything runs smoothly.

Corrie and her dance partner, Frank Finesse (cerebellum), make a wonderful couple. If she becomes unwell she loses her beautiful, flowing movements and actually slows down and shakes or sometimes loses control of her movements.

Further reading

Graybiel, A.M. and Rauch, S.L. (2000) 'Toward a neurobiology of obsessive-compulsive disorder.' *Neuron 28*, 343–347.

Kalat, J.W. (2004) *Biological Psychology* (8th edition). Victoria: Thomson Wadsworth.

Skarderud, F. (2006) 'Force of Habit.' In Anne-Sofie Hjemdahl (Ed.) *A Thing or Two about Ibsen*, pp. 151–160. Oslo: Andrimne.

Winston, R. (2003) *The Human Mind and How to Make the Most of it*. Sydney: Bantam.

Chapter 16

Felicity Feelall: the Thalamus

Meet Felicity Feelall

Felicity Feelall lives on Pleasure Island in the very middle of Lake Tertius (third ventricle). This lies in the heart of Midtown Cephalton, under the span of the Mainbridge (body of corpus callosum) on Christopher Crosstalk's (corpus callosum) property. It may appear that she is isolated, surrounded as she is by the very tranquil waters of the lake, but in fact all routes in Cephalton seem to lead to Felicity's home. Here is her famous polysensory clinic that she runs as a 'masseuse and sensory psychotherapist'. Major highways and minor pathways, from Uptown Cephalton to the southernmost parts of the Shire, all converge on Pleasure Island, which seems strangely misnamed considering the negative experiences of pain and suffering that are brought there by so many of those she treats. The only way onto the island is via tunnels that emerge on different parts of the island.

Felicity is a big, strong curvaceous woman who, though almost completely grey, is still very sensual. She runs the polysensory clinic for all those who want to be in touch with their feelings and who want a listening ear, a perceptive eye and the touch that can detect pain. In fact, many prominent Cephalton figures have weekends and holiday houses on Pleasure Island and have personal links with Felicity, with whom they stay in close touch. Both Corrie O'Graphie (basal ganglia) and Frank Finesse (cerebellum) have contributed to Felicity's eurythmic or

169

movement therapy, even though it is the sensory side of the clinic's work that has received most public attention.

Felicity talks frequently with the town leadership – Fredrick Foresight (frontal lobes), Rochelle Ringbond (cingulate gyrus) and Dudley Doit (motor cortex).

She is very close to Christopher Crosstalk, her secret admirer and close neighbour, and they have many friends in common. He is always hovering over her and, like him, she is very public minded and always has time for listening. When she doesn't know the answer to someone's problem she puts people in touch with each other for help, just as Christopher does. They differ in that Felicity has more 'out of town friends' whilst Christopher tends to link up with those in town itself. Some say that she is closer to Tony Turnon (locus coeruleus) than Rosie Reaction (autonomic nervous system) would like. But the truth is that Tony and Felicity are just good friends who have a tendency to keep each other activated and focused when they work together.

Felicity uses all of the senses therapeutically for her patients – massage therapies, phototherapy, music therapy, tactile and eurythmic therapies. She provides a level of awareness in Cephalton, both of the town itself and the Shire beyond, which enables the town and Shire to think of itself as a single entity. She is like a huge spotlight in the darkness. Whatever she shines on becomes the focus for the whole community. Knowing almost immediately what is happening and where it is happening as a result of picking up vibes from throughout the Shire, and feeling the temperature of every situation and listening to the pain and suffering of all those who come to her clinic, enable Felicity to pass on such important information. She seems to have the capacity to keep the whole town alert to what is going on and no-one is quite sure how she does it.

It can sometimes be hard to know how Felicity herself feels given that she is so busy dealing with everyone else and that she has never been one for words. It can be difficult to register when she herself is not well. Signs of her being ill are when the problems of others are not being registered by the community; when those who should know are unaware; when the pain of different parts of the community goes unregistered;

when the leaders of Cephalton do not pick up the vibes and temperature of community concern; when there is a loss of that light touch that is so needed in so many situations to finesse progress and prevent harm to the whole community; and especially when feelings in the Shire are not relayed to those in charge.

The thalamus explained

Location and structure

The word thalamus comes from the Greek word *thalamos*, which means anteroom, inner chamber or bridal bedroom. The thalamus is situated in the centre of the brain just underneath the cerebral hemispheres and the corpus callosum and above the hypothalamus. The thalamus, approximately 4 cm in length, is made up of two egg-shaped bulbs of grey matter cells that look a little like two avocados joined side by side. It has several sections, the anterior (northern end of Pleasure Island), medial (middle of Pleasure Island), posterior (southern part of Pleasure Island) and lateral parts (eastern and western shoreline) with collections of nuclei in each section.

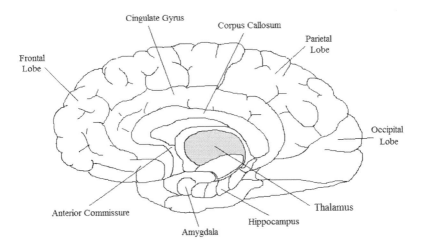

Figure 16.1. Medial view (inner surface) of the right side of the brain showing the thalamus shaded in grey.

Connections

The thalamus has numerous connections, with inputs from the spinal cord, cerebellum and the basal ganglia, and outputs to the amygdala, periaqueductal grey matter, hippocampus, insula, and the whole of the motor and sensory cortex.

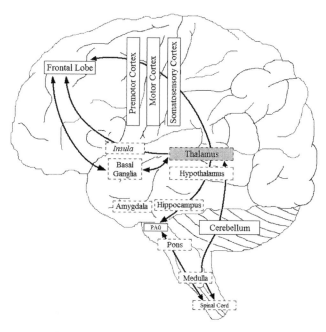

Figure 16.2. Lateral view (outer surface) of the left side of the brain, showing a schematic representation of the main connections of the thalamus. Note the intimate relationship between the thalamus, the somatosensory cortex, the insula and the PAG – Periaqueductal grey matter.

Functions

The thalamus has three important functions:

- Filtering and focusing pain and other sensations
- Relaying pain and sensation to the subcortex and cortex
- Integrating movement and sensation

FILTERING AND FOCUSING OF ALL SENSATION INCLUDING PAIN

There is an immense amount of sensory information converging on the brain, both from the environment and the rest of the body. Consequently the ability to deal with it both unconsciously and consciously is constrained. The thalamus functions a little like a spotlight, directing attention and information to those areas of interest. It plays a major part in the initial filtering of sensory stimuli, including pain, before relaying to other areas of the subcortex and cortex in a more discriminating manner. For example, in relation to pain, the thalamus sets the threshold for how much is relayed upwards; in other words, pain is generally reduced to becoming a signal rather than a handicap. This filtering provides an initial focus for determining the importance of the sensory stimulus. After this information is relayed to, and processed by, the subcortex and cortex (see below), it is sent back to the thalamus for more detailed analysis. This interchange between the thalamus, subcortex and cortex enables a more sophisticated processing of the stimulus.

RELAYING SENSATION, INCLUDING PAIN, TO THE SUBCORTEX AND CORTEX

Having filtered pain and sensation, the thalamus relays this information to the subcortex and cortex for further processing. Subcortical structures provide a quick scan for emotional threat (amygdala) and a quick response for pain overload (periaqueductal grey matter). Cortical structures provide a more detailed analysis of the information relayed from the thalamus. For example, visual sensation is relayed to the occipital cortex and auditory sensation is relayed to the temporal cortex, each for further processing. The 'conversation' between thalamus, subcortex and cortex continues back and forth.

INTEGRATING MOVEMENT AND SENSATION

As well as relaying pain and sensation the thalamus is also involved in relaying information relevant to movement. It does this by conveying information from the cerebellum and basal ganglia to the premotor and motor cortex for the preparation of movement, thus ensuring that every movement is an accurate response to the sensations received.

When things go wrong

Thalamic dysfunction is rare. When it does occur the principal manifestations are pain, paraesthesia and hallucinations.

PAIN

Such pain is out of proportion to the stimulus and consequently disabling. This is best illustrated by the central pain syndrome, a rare neurological disorder occurring after thalamic damage. It is characterised by hypersensitivity to pain, due to the lowered pain threshold, and is sometimes experienced as intolerable with burning, tearing or searing sensations. In turn, the pain is exacerbated by exposure to heat/cold or emotional distress.

PARAESTHESIAE

Paraesthesiae are defined as altered sensations, including tingling, crawling feelings beneath the skin or pain and temperature alterations in the skin, unrelated to the environment.

HALLUCINATIONS

Hallucinations are due to the relaying of false information, mainly to the auditory or visual cortex.

Technical corner

The thalamus, like the cingulate gyrus (see Chapter 3), plays an important part in *attention*. This it does through its continuing 'conversation' with the subcortex and cortex. Attention is distinguished from *concentration*, which is the ability to attend over a period of time. Finally, the experience of this process is *consciousness*.

Summarising Felicity Feelall

Felicity is the heart and bosom of Cephalton and the Shire around. All routes lead to Pleasure Island, where she lives, and many of Cephalton's best and brightest have places on the island and links to the vital therapeutic work that she does in the polysensory clinic. She does so much in Cephalton and the Shire that is easy to overlook – an almost invisible function of keeping everyone in touch with what is happening. She generates a large part of the community's consciousness of what it is to live in Cephalton. She is very active in making sure that important information is relayed to the most appropriate community members. She is also able to focus on important things and helps Fredrick Foresight (frontal lobes) and Rochelle Ringbond to maintain focus on such important things as well. She is not only interested in sensory therapies but is also deeply involved in integrating movement therapies into treatment.

When Felicity feels unwell, there can be a failure of those normally in the know, to be aware of community feeling and pain in different regions of the Shire. Or sometimes, because Felicity is not able to guide them, those in charge can misread what is going on or react to false information.

Further reading

Blumenfeld, H. (2002) *Neuroanatomy through Clinical Cases*. Sunderland, MA: Sinauer Associates.

Mesulam, M.M. (2000) *Principles of Behavioural and Cognitive Neurology*, 2nd edition. New York, NY: Oxford University Press.

Nestler, E.J., Hyman, S.E. and Malenka, R.C. (2001) *Molecular Neuropharmacology – A Foundation for Clinical Neuroscience*. New York, NY: McGraw Hill, pp. 255–276.

Chapter 17

Uma Underbride and Horace Hormone: the Hypothalamus and Pituitary

Meet Uma Underbride and Horace Hormone

Uma Underbride and Horace Hormone live very close to each other by Lake Tertius (third ventricle) in the Turkish Saddle Canyon (sella turcica). Uma's place is on the southern crest, just above Horace Hormone's hideaway. She is the head of emergency services for Cephalton and the Shire, and Horace is the town pharmacist. Uma and Horace are intimately involved with each other. She asks and he does. She is the question and he is the answer. She is the command and he is the response.

Uma reads the temperature of each situation and then responds to the chemistry of the moment. Generally she keeps a steady hand on any situation by maintaining the status quo. However, when Annie Almond (amygdala) indicates the presence of a threat, Uma passes on any vital information to Horace, who listens carefully and then sends pharmaceuticals around the Shire as required. At the same time, Rosie Reaction (autonomic nervous system) instantly communicates her concerns to the

Shire. They are all working in tandem, with Uma as the leader, and Horace responding as if he is using 'snail mail' and Rosie as if with email. Together Uma and Horace also look to the future, promote the growth of the town and the Shire and aim toward steady expansion.

Beside Annie, Uma also listens to the views of Brenda Bridgehead (insula) and associates of Penelope Panorama (optic tracts) and in turn talks to Rosie Reaction, Fay Faceandear (pons) and Sam Swallowtalk (medulla). Horace, however, has no direct connections with others in Cephalton, beside Uma.

When Uma is unwell this can have profound effects on the whole of Cephalton and the Shire. The community can become destabilised by even minor problems, let alone emergencies. Threats to smooth running of services can so upset the community that people feel far less secure and have difficulty sleeping and eating.

When Horace is unwell the health, growth and expansion of the whole population can be affected. He becomes erratic and inappropriately sends medicines around the Shire, and, when very ill, may not provide even those medicines required for emergencies.

Location and structure

The hypothalamus is located in the floor of the third ventricle, below the thalamus, and immediately above the pituitary. It is composed of many nuclei, is about the size of a thumb nail and weighs about four grams.

The pituitary sits in a bony saddle, the sella turcica, immediately posterior to the optic chiasm, above and anterior to the brain stem. It is made up of an anterior and pituitary section and is the size of a large pea, weighing about 1–2 grams.

Connections

The hypothalamus and pituitary are integrally connected with each other. The hypothalamus has input from the amygdala, insula and the optic tracts and outputs to the autonomic nervous system in the pons and

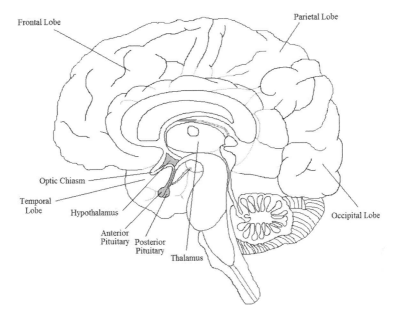

Figure 17.1. Medial view (inner surface) of the right side of the brain showing the hypothalamus and pituitary, shaded in grey. Each of the visible main lobes of the brain is labelled.

medulla. The pituitary, which has no other neuronal connections, communicates with other organs in the body through the release of hormones.

Functions

The hypothalamus and pituitary serve three major functions:

- Emergency response to threat
- Promotion of homeostasis
- Growth and reproduction

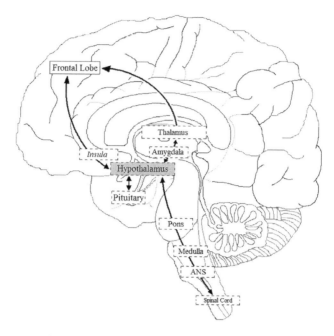

Figure 17.2. Medial view (inner surface) of the right side of the brain showing a schematic representation of the main connections of the hypothalamus and pituitary. Note the exclusive relationship between the hypothalamus and pituitary. Note also the proximity of the amygdala (threat detector for the sympathetic system) and the insula (main command centre for the parasympathetic system) to the hypothalamus (chief activator of the automatic nervous system (ANS)).

EMERGENCY RESPONSE TO THREAT

Activating the sympathetic nervous system (SNS)

When an external threat is identified by the amygdala, information is relayed to the hypothalamus, which in turn activates a rapid response from the sympathetic nervous system of fright, fight and flight.

Activation of hormonal stress response

In contrast to the rapid SNS response to threat, there is a slower but longer-lasting response. This involves the release of a chemical messenger/hormone, corticotropin releasing hormone (CTH), which triggers the pituitary to release adrenocorticotropin hormone (ACTH). This in turn stimulates the adrenal gland to release cortisol, which increases the body's capacity to handle stress by making more energy available. Sufficient cortisol over time then feeds back to the hypothalamus and switches off the stress response.

PROMOTION OF HOMEOSTASIS

Activation of the parasympathetic nervous system (PNS)

When an internal change in the body is identified by the insula, information is relayed to the hypothalamus. This in turn activates a rapid response from the parasympathetic nervous system of calm, rest and digest.

Regulation of body temperature

The body operates normally within a narrow temperature range (36–38 degrees centigrade). This range may be threatened by external or internal events. External events involve changes in the environmental temperature and internal events involve changes due to certain disease processes, e.g. hypo- or hyperthyroidism. The hypothalamus provides constancy of body temperature by sending a message from its heat-sensitive cells to the ANS to encourage a balance between SNS and PNS activity.

Regulation of body activities

The needs of the body trigger the hypothalamus and pituitary to regulate essential activities such as eating, drinking and sleep.

Regulation of body chemistry

There are a number of centres within the hypothalamus and pituitary which detect changes in body chemistry, such as levels of sodium and potassium or acidity and alkalinity. In response to such changes, messages are sent via hormones to the kidneys to adjust the chemical imbalances.

GROWTH AND REPRODUCTION

Growth and reproduction are orchestrated by the hypothalamus and pituitary through the production and circulation of hormones to various organs in the body (see Table 17.1). This process consists of four phases:

1. Activation of hormone production – hypothalamus

2. Production of hormones – pituitary

3. Secretion of hormones – pituitary

4. Feedback from target organs to hypothalamus

When things go wrong

There are three conditions that illustrate what can go wrong.

HYPOTHALAMIC SYNDROME

This rare condition is due to inflammation, tumour or autoimmune disease, with consequent erratic activity which may be increased or decreased or both. It impairs homeostasis, and therefore such basic activities as appetite, thirst and sleep. It most commonly manifests as extreme hunger, thirst and sleepiness with excessive aggression due to overactivation of the hypothalamus. However, the opposite may occur with decreased eating, thirst and sleep, and with apathy, due to underactivation of the hypothalamus.

> Carl, aged three, suddenly started drinking large amounts of fluid and passing large amounts of urine. This was accompanied by eating ravenously and indiscriminately, with consequent 90 per cent increase in weight over a three-week period. In addition he was extremely anxious and aggressive to his family. Between these episodes he would sleep 16 hours a day. Over the next three months, his symptoms exacerbated and he subsequently died. A postmortem examination showed inflammation around the hypothalamus, pituitary and amygdala, due to an auto-immune reaction.

Table 17.1. Hormones produced in the hypothalamus and pituitary

Growth hormone releasing factor	Hypothalamus	Stimulates release of growth hormone from the pituitary
Gonadotropin releasing hormone	Hypothalamus	Stimulates release of luteinising hormone + follicle stimulating hormone from the pituitary
Thyrotropin releasing hormone	Hypothalamus	Stimulates release of thyroid stimulating hormone from the pituitary
Corticotropin releasing hormone	Hypothalamus	Stimulates release of adrenocorticotropin hormone from the pituitary
Prolactin inhibiting factor (Dopamine)	Hypothalamus	Inhibits release of prolactin from the pituitary
Growth hormone	Pituitary	Promotes growth
Luteinising hormone and follicle stimulating hormone	Pituitary	Ovarian development and activity
Thyroid stimulating hormone	Pituitary	Stimulates thyroid to produce thyroxine (thyroid hormone)
Adrenocorticotropin hormone	Pituitary	Stimulates adrenal gland to produce cortisol
Prolactin	Pituitary	Stimulates the breasts to produce milk
Oxytocin	Pituitary	Stimulates contraction of the uterus during the monthly cycle and in labour
Antidiuretic hormone (vasopressin)	Pituitary	Suppresses urine production during the night

This case demonstrates disturbances in some of the key functions of the hypothalamus including bodily homeostasis and the emergency response to threat.

HYPOPITUITARISM

This usually arises as a result of a tumour suppressing pituitary activity by encroachment on hormone-producing cells. Hypopituitarism manifests with decreased growth, hypothyroidism, impaired stress response, and lack of sexual development.

HYPERPITUITARISM

This is also usually due to a tumour with production of large amounts of hormones. It manifests with excessive growth (acromegaly and gigantism), hyperthyroidism, excess stress response and excess production of sex hormones with consequent disruption of normal menstrual cycle, and changes in sexual characteristics and behaviour.

The classic pituitary case: Goliath the philistine

The story of David and Goliath from the Old Testament suggests that Goliath was over three metres tall. The most likely explanation for this is that he suffered from hyperpituitarism, leading to extreme height and large jaw, hands and feet. Such stature is often associated with clumsiness and lack of agility. In contrast David's normal size would have enabled him to move with precision and agility.

Technical corner

The dexamethasone suppression test is a test of the ability of the hypothalamus to turn off the stress response when sufficient cortisol is available. In major anxiety and depression, even high cortisol levels will not switch off the hypothalamic stress response. This can be tested by administering artificial cortisol (dexamethasone). If there is no lowering of serum cortisol levels this indicates a failure of the hypothalamus to turn off the stress response, due to chronic hypothalamic overactivity.

Uma Underbride and Horace Hormone in summary

Uma and Horace, living by Lake Tertius, share an intimate personal and work life. Between them they are vital to the smooth running of Cephalton and the Shire beyond. They provide responses to threat, promote balance and harmony within the Shire and ensure reasonable growth and development. When things go wrong there is a destabilisation of basic activities across the Shire and particularly alterations in appetite, sleep and bodily rhythms, as well as effects on the health, growth and expansion of the whole community.

Further reading

Blumenfeld, H. (2002) *Neuroanatomy through Clinical Cases*. Sunderland, MA: Sinauer.

Nunn, K., Ouvrier, R., Sprague, T., Arbuckle, S. and Docker, M. (1997) 'Idiopathic hypothalamic dysfunction: A paraneoplastic syndrome?' *Journal of Child Neurology 12*, 4, 276–281.

Part Four

The Brain Stem, Cerebellum and Beyond

Chapter 18

Fay Faceandear and Sam Swallowtalk: the Pons and Medulla

Meet Fay Faceandear and Sam Swallowtalk

Fay Faceandear (pons) and Sam Swallowtalk (medulla), intimate friends and neighbours, live in Downtown Cephalton. Fay's place is just below Felicity Feelall's (thalamus) property, above Sam's and in front of Frank Finesse (cerebellum). Sam lives below Fay and Frank but above Rosie Reaction (autonomic nervous system) and the Downtown Dream Team (reticular formation).

Fay is the 'the face and ears of Cephalton'. She owns the Narrow Bridge Cafe, the main internet café in Downtown, situated next to the Cephalton power station. The café is the conduit for much news about what is happening in Cephalton and the Shire. Fay will often find out what is happening in the Shire and the outside world before those in charge.

Sam, Fay's most intimate friend, is an engineer who is Director of the Cephalton power station. He literally keeps Cephalton going so that all business and every home in Cephalton and the Shire is supplied with electricity. There is a standing joke in Cephalton that, without Sam, no-one could eat, speak or sleep. He keeps the business, and therefore the town, of Cephalton alive.

They both have many friends, including Dudley Doit, Felicity Feelall, Frank Finesse and the Downtown Dream Team (reticular formation), most of whom live on one or other of their properties. But, being the last properties in Cephalton before the Shire begins, both Fay and Sam communicate a great deal with those who are most closely connected with the Shire, like Rosie Reaction (autonomic nervous system).

Fay and Sam are so close to one another that the mood or health of one invariably has a profound effect on the other. Without the communication of the café with the Shire and the rest of Cephalton there is a total disconnection between the town and the Shire. Without the power supply from the power station, almost everything ceases. If this continued for any length of time, the whole town would be in danger of total collapse – an urban corpse.

The pons and medulla explained

Location and structure

The pons (Latin for bridge) is above the medulla and below the thalamus (see Figure 18.1). It is a densely packed convergence of nuclei and pathways. The medulla is located at the base of the skull (foramen magnum) below the pons and above the spinal cord. Both are surrounded by cerebrospinal fluid.

Connections

The pons and medulla have input from: (a) the motor cortex, (b) the thalamus, (c) the hypothalamus, (d) the cerebellum, (e) the fifth, seventh, eighth, ninth and tenth cranial nerves, and (f) the autonomic nervous system, reticular formation and the spinal cord. They have output to: (a) the whole cerebral cortex, (b) the thalamus, (c) the hypothalamus, (d) the cerebellum, (e) the fifth, sixth, seventh, ninth, tenth, eleventh and twelfth cranial nerves, and (f) the autonomic nervous system, reticular formation and the spinal cord (see Figure 18.2).

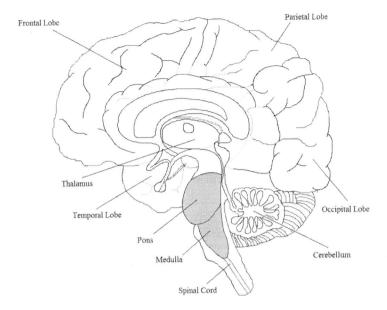

Figure 18.1. Medial view (inner surface) of the right side of the brain showing the pons and medulla shaded in grey. Each of the visible main lobes of the brain, is labelled.

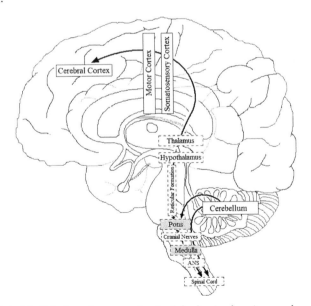

Figure 18.2. Medial view (inner surface) of the brain showing a schematic representation of the main connections of the pons and medulla. Note the reticular formation actually goes through the core of both pons and medulla rather than sitting on top, as represented here. The pons and medulla provide an opportunity for the cerebellum to have input to all information that goes up and down the brain stem.

Functions

The main functions of the pons and medulla are:

- Networking between the cerebral cortex, thalamus and the cerebellum

- Relaying sensation from the body to the thalamus and messages from the cortex to the body

- The pons and medulla are also involved in regulating such basic functions as heart rate, breathing, sleep and waking, and pain control (these functions are covered in more detail in Chapter 20 – autonomic nervous system and reticular formation)

- The pons specialises in relaying sensation from the face to the thalamus and messages from the motor cortex to the face.

- The medulla specialises in relaying sensation involving speech and swallowing from the tongue and throat to the thalamus, and relaying messages from the motor cortex back to the tongue and throat – this includes the vomiting reflex

When things go wrong

The strategic position of the pons and medulla means that considerable problems can occur when there is even a small area of damage or dysfunction. These include: stroke, tumour, trauma, infection and demyelination. Any of these can lead to disconnection between the cerebral cortex, thalamus, cerebellum and spinal cord. This in turn can lead to problems with consciousness, facial sensation and movement, body sensation, gross and fine movement, and balance. In addition, specific to the medulla, would be problems with swallowing and vital functions such as heart rate and breathing.

A TUMOUR

> Linda, 29, woke up one morning with blurred vision, and when she looked in the mirror, her left eye was fixed to one side. The next day she was unrousable and was urgently hospitalised. MRI revealed an inoperable tumour in the pons extending into the medulla. Although she woke for brief periods during the next three weeks she slowly lost eye and facial movements and the ability to swallow; eventually became totally paralysed and comatose. Her breathing and heart rate became slow and irregular and she died shortly after.

This case illustrates the devastating impact of a tumour in such a critical position as the pons and medulla. Abnormal eye movements and difficulties with swallowing are often the first signs of a problem in this area. The paralysis resulting from the interruption in the motor pathways and the irregularities in breathing and heart rate was due to compression of the cardiorespiratory centres in the medulla. The impaired consciousness resulted from interruption of the pathways between the medulla, pons and the cerebral cortex.

MULTIPLE SCLEROSIS

> Jason, ten, reported blurred vision and over the next four years he had five episodes during which he had problems with seeing, talking and moving, from which he only partially recovered. At the age of 14 a further episode led to an inability to talk or walk but he was clearly conscious. Over the next few days he regained his speech and was able to convey the terror he experienced in being 'locked in' and his fear of recurrence. After extensive investigation, which revealed demyelination within the pons and medulla, he was diagnosed with multiple sclerosis. Despite treatment six months later he went into coma and died.

This case illustrates the profound impact of disconnection between the motor cortex and the rest of the body, as a result of demyelination in the pons and medulla, whilst consciousness remains fully intact. As the disease progressed those centres involved with vital functions became affected and led to his death.

MOEBIUS SYNDROME

A specific example of a cranial nerve abnormality in the pons is that of Moebius syndrome. This is manifested by a complete lack of facial movement due to a failure of the facial nerve to stimulate the muscles of the face. Moebius syndrome is a very rare condition that involves the underdevelopment of the nuclei of the sixth and seventh cranial nerves, located in the pons. This condition prevents any facial movement, including that conveying emotion. It is therefore difficult for observers to know what the sufferer is experiencing. The condition might be suspected in infancy because of an inability to suck or smile.

Technical corner

The 12 cranial nerves carry out the following functions:

1. Olfactory nerve	Smell
2. Ophthalmic nerve	Vision
3. Oculomotor nerve	Eye movement, pupillary size and focusing
4. Trochlear nerve	Eye movement
5. Trigeminal nerve	Chewing and facial sensation
6. Abducens nerve	Eye movement
7. Facial nerve	Facial movement; taste at front of the tongue; tear production and salivation
8. Auditory nerve	Hearing and balance
9. Glossopharyngeal nerve and salivation	Swallowing, taste at back of tongue
10. Vagal nerve	Parasympathetic communication to the chest and abdomen; laryngeal movement

11. Accessory nerve   Head and shoulder movement

12. Hypoglossal nerve   Tongue movement

Fay Faceandear and Sam Swallowtalk in summary

Fay and Sam, a loving and very hardworking couple, living in Downtown Cephalton, are vital to the everyday life, and to the actual life, of Cephalton and the Shire. Through their management of the internet café and the power station they ensure efficient and effective two-way communication and all the vital functions of any community. Without their full involvement life is threatened.

Further reading

Blumenfeld, H. (2002) *Neuroanatomy through Clinical Cases.* Sunderland, MA: Sinauer.

Ouanounou, S., Saigal, G. and Birchansky, S. (2005) 'Mobius syndrome.' *American Journal of Neuroradiology 26*, 430–432.

Chapter 19

Frank Finesse: the Cerebellum

Meet Frank Finesse

Frank Finesse lives in Downtown Cephalton on a massive and relatively isolated property which, despite its hills and dales, is almost half as big as the rest of Cephalton put together. It is located just next to the amazing underground Lake Diamond (fourth ventricle) fed by Sylvian streams from Lake Tertius (third ventricle). The property lies behind the home of Fay Faceandear (pons), above that of her partner, Sam Swallowtalk (medulla), and overlooked by Penelope Panorama's estate (occipital lobes). Along with Fay and Sam, Frank is one of the oldest residents of Cephalton. However, he remains impressively fit and into all things athletic.

Although Frank lives alone, he has contact with a very wide range of people throughout the town. He, and his old flame and best friend, Corrie O'Graphie (basal ganglia), still lead the ballroom dancing classes in town, leaving younger members like Fredrick Foresight (frontal lobes) and Dudley Doit (motor cortex) looking quite ungainly. They may decide on, and be in charge of, all of the action in the town, but Frank makes it happen with accuracy and on time.

He is a stickler for detail and no dance step goes unscrutinised. Corrie explains the sequences and Frank focuses on style, poise and precision.

Frank is a strange mix. He is a man of habit and routine but he also keeps in touch, learns quickly and lets everyone else in turn know it, making sure that others take on board the latest dance moves while not forgetting the old ones.

Earlier in his life he travelled with a circus and did high-wire balancing acts. Even now his feats of balance and riding on horses at the local rodeo still amaze much younger men. There is always a sense in which Frank surprises everyone with hidden skills. He seems solitary, but in fact social events take on a whole new dimension when he is about. When things look out of step, he soon fixes them so they are back on track. He collects clocks and maps for a hobby and loves working on them. Frank is as accurate with his clocks and pernickety with his maps as he is with his dancing. He is very attentive to the finest detail but can then shift his focus to his outdoor work very quickly when needed. He prides himself on being a senior member of the community and likes to help in every aspect of the activities of the town.

Frank has one weakness, in that he does not handle alcohol very well and becomes drunk much more quickly than most others in town. Suddenly, with just a few drinks, Frank is a mess – 'paralytic' as his friends would say – staggering and slurred in his speech. It is something Frank prefers not to talk about.

The cerebellum explained

Location and structure

The cerebellum is located at the back of the brain, behind the brain stem, below the occipital lobes and above the spinal cord. Although some say it looks a little like a cauliflower, it also looks like a second, smaller brain, which is what the word cerebellum means. Between the cerebellum and the brain stem is the fourth ventricle (Lake Diamond). Above the cerebellum is a small tent of tough and thick tissue known as the tentorium cerebelli (tent of the cerebellum).

In adult life the cerebellum is about the size of a person's fist and weighs about 150 g – one-tenth the size of the rest of the brain. The

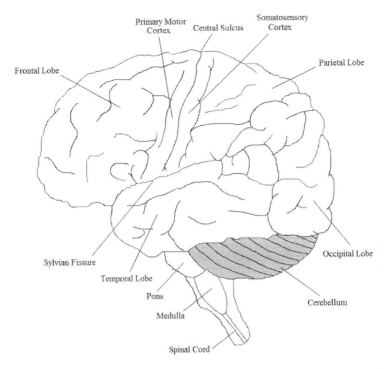

Figure 19.1. Lateral view (outer surface) of the left side of the brain showing the cerebellum shaded in grey. Each of the visible main lobes of the brain is labelled.

cerebellum has a remarkable amount of folds, which conceal its true size. Its actual surface area exceeds that of one hemisphere of the cortex and it contains 50 per cent of the neurones in the entire brain, in a highly compressed form.

Like the rest of the brain, the cerebellum has two hemispheres made up of white matter on the inside, with grey matter on the outside. These hemispheres are joined by the vermis (literally meaning 'worm') and have their own maps of the body, especially the limbs, and also maps of the body in space as indicated by sound and vision.

Connections

The cerebellum has an enormous number of connections, too complex to mention in any detail, but most significantly with the basal ganglia and the frontal lobes, necessary for its multitudinous functions (see below). There are three main points of contact or peduncles (Greek for footings) – the superior, middle and inferior cerebellar peduncles – connecting the cerebellum to the pons and medulla. These all have inputs and outputs with many parts of the brain via the pons and medulla.

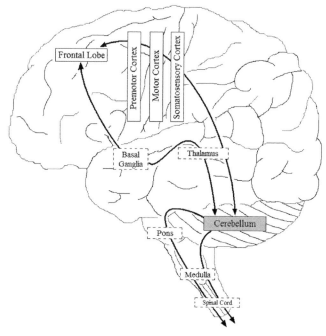

Figure 19.2. Lateral view (outer surface) of the brain showing a schematic representation of the main connections of the cerebellum. Note the close relationship between the brain stem and the thalamus, and the cerebellum.

Functions

The cerebellum has three main functions:

- Coordinating movement and balance
- Fine tuning movement
- Integrating sensory, motor and cognitive functioning

SENSORY, ENABLING COORDINATION OF MOVEMENT AND BALANCE

The cerebellum receives and processes sensory information from throughout the body, via the thalamus, spinal cord, pons and medulla, with the specific purpose of maintaining balance and preparing the trunk, shoulders and hips for movement. Having processed this sensory information, the cerebellum communicates with those brain structures, such as the motor cortex and the basal ganglia, most significantly involved with movement (see below).

FINE TUNING MOTOR MOVEMENT

Although not initiating movement, the cerebellum plans, monitors and regulates the progress of both reflex and voluntary movements. It is involved in fine movements, balance and any new movements that require effort to learn.

INTEGRATION OF SENSORY, MOTOR AND COGNITIVE FUNCTIONING

Although this aspect of cerebellar function is not as yet clearly understood, it does seem to aid the integration of sensory information with cognitive function and motor activity. This allows for the timing and sequencing of movement in relation to mood and conscious thought. Examples include such activities as speech, dancing or the playing of a musical instrument.

When things go wrong

Cerebellar dysfunction is associated with many conditions which affect balance, fine movement, and the learning of new movements. Common causes include alcohol misuse, many medications, cerebral anoxia and vertebrobasilar insufficiency.

THE CEREBELLAR SYNDROME

The cerebellar syndrome (Table 19.1) illustrates what can happen clinically in cerebellar dysfunction. Common features include tremors, incoordination and loss of balance. There are associated rapid, ballistic movement sequences (arms or legs may move unpredictably, powerfully and suddenly – like a gun going off) that require precise aiming, accurate trajectory and timing. There is difficulty with fine movements such as typing, tapping a rhythm, pointing at a moving object, speaking, writing, playing musical instruments, athletic activities and even hand-clapping (Kalat, 2004).

Table 19.1. The cerebellar syndrome

1. Disturbed balance
Wide-based gait
Tendency to fall over
Sensation of spinning or vertigo
Difficulty managing balance when eyes closed

2. Loss of muscle tone
Pendular limb reflexes
Hyperextensible joints
Snoring (reduced soft palate muscle tone)
Flopping feet when walking

3. Motor incoordination
Slurring of speech
Nystagmus (eyeball flickers horizontally)
Diminished smooth muscular movement
Ataxia (difficulty walking)

CEREBELLAR ANOXIA

The cerebellum is one of the first brain structures to be affected by lack of oxygen, its Purkinje cells being amongst the most sensitive in the brain to oxygen starvation.

Justin, two and a half years old, had fallen into the family swimming pool when he was 14 months old. It took four minutes to resuscitate him. He had a very noticeable nystagmus, walked with his legs wide apart and shook vigorously whenever he tried to do something.

These symptoms are clearly a result of oxygen deprivation to the cerebellum.

ALCOHOL MISUSE

The cerebellum is one of the first brain structures to be affected by alcohol, as manifested by poor coordination. Simple tests for drunkenness include assessing fine movements such as the ability to walk a straight line or touch the nose with a finger ('finger-to-nose test' – see technical corner). Such tests are also used medically when seeking evidence of cerebellar damage.

VERTEBROBASILAR INSUFFICIENCY

There are three main vessels which provide circulation to the back of the brain: the two vertebral arteries and one basilar artery. The hindbrain (including the cerebellum) is the first part of the brain to be affected by lack of supply of blood or oxygen. The most common way that a lack of blood supply occurs in this area is when cholesterol accumulates in a blood vessel wall over many years preventing blood from flowing freely through the vessels. The administration of aspirin each day can assist in preventing blood clotting, but left untreated a stroke may well ensue.

Yvonne, a 70-year-old widow, lived alone in a retirement village. She had been experiencing episodic bouts of dizziness and fainting. She had extensive investigations which revealed obstructions in the vertebral and basilar arteries with subsequent clotting of the blood supply to the cerebellum. The obstructions were due to cholesterol plaque and treatment with aspirin significantly reduced these episodes.

The classic cerebellum case: a physician diagnoses himself

Gaspard Vieusseux, a nineteenth-century Swiss physician, noted he had episodes of dizziness, nystagmus (jerking eyes), difficulties in swallowing and speaking clearly, marked tremor, inability to gauge temperature or feel pain on one side of his face, and a tendency to fall toward that side. He concluded that one of the key arteries to the cerebellum (posterior inferior cerebellar artery) was becoming intermittently blocked. Subsequently he named it the posterior inferior cerebellar artery syndrome (PICA).

Technical corner

During the finger-to-nose test, subjects are asked to hold an arm out straight and then to touch their nose with their finger as quickly as possible. Normal subjects would first move their fingers smoothly and quickly to a point just in front of their noses, then touch their nose, and finally withdraw the finger with a slower movement. Those subjects with cerebellar damage or alcohol misuse may have difficulties with many aspects of this test. The finger may show a coarse tremor, stop too soon or go too far, hitting the nose, or missing it and touching another part of the face (Kalat 2004).

Frank Finesse in summary

Frank, one of the older members of the community, lives alone on his large estate in Downtown Cephalton. Despite his age he is remarkably fit and agile and continues to enjoy dancing with his best friend, Corrie O'Graphie. He is a stickler for accuracy of movement and leads the town in his ability to learn new skills. When unwell he tends to lose his balance, coordination and muscle tone.

Reference

Kalat, J.W. (2004) *Biological Psychology* (8th Edition). Victoria: Thomson Wadsworth.

Further reading

Bower, J.M. and Parsons, L.M. (2003) 'Rethinking the "lesser brain".' *Scientific American*, August, 40–47.

Gazzaniga, M.S., Ivry, R.B. and Mangun, G.R. (2007) *Cognitive Neuroscience: The Biology of the Mind* (2nd edition). New York, NY: Norton.

Chapter 20

Rosie Reaction and the Downtown Dream Team: the Autonomic Nervous System (ANS) and the Reticular Formation (RF)

Meet Rosie Reaction and the Downtown Dream Team

Rosie Reaction does not really have a home of her own, but tends to move from one member of the family to another, depending upon what is happening around her and how she is feeling within herself. Her relatives are scattered everywhere – in Downtown Cephalton and particularly along both sides of the long mountain range, below Cephalton, the Somite Mountains (vertebral column).

The calmer members of her family (parasympathetic nervous system) tend to live in Downtown Cephalton and at the southern end of the Somite mountain range (sacral spine). They are quieter and try to avoid excitement. They like the rhythms of daily living and change is not their favourite word. They are traditionalists and conservatives, and work hard to keep things the same as they have always been.

The more excitable members of the Reaction family (sympathetic nervous system) also live along the mountain range (in the thoracic and lumbar regions), not as far south as the relaxed Reactions, but in the region just below Cephalton (cervical spine). They tend to be highly strung, adventure and thrill-seeking, action-loving and altogether ready to take on the challenges of change.

Rosie is integrally involved with both sides of her family and, in some ways, a strange mix of both. She feels the pain, the pulse, the breath, the gut-wrenching struggles and the exhilaration of those around her, from within the town itself to the outermost parts of the Shire, wherever her family lives or has connections.

As part of the Cephalton Emergency Services, led by Uma Underbride (hypothalamus), she is there in flood and fire and ready to help the community whether in 'fight or flight', in order to protect it. She and Uma work beautifully together. Uma stands back, after balancing the information coming in, and gives the orders, often after Annie Almond (amygdala) has raised the general alarm. But Rosie gets as close to the action as she can. Her ability to mobilise the community in a very short time is extraordinary.

Like Uma, Rosie is not one for talk. Both are concerned to affect the community at its grass roots and to do it quickly in response to need. In emergencies, Rosie can become mobilised within an instant. And when she is aroused, she is so in every way – in mind, in flesh and in blood. While other people *talk* about being angry, she is plunged into the *experience* of heart-heaving, breath-gasping, pupils dilating, skin-blanching, fists clenching and teeth-baring. She can be quite frightening, even formidable. At such times, Rosie does not think about food, drink, sleep or any of her own daily needs. She is alert, focused, invigorated and mobilised to the full. Rosie gets a real adrenaline rush when she is in the thick of action.

It was in the midst of an emergency that she met Tony Turnon (locus coeruleus), one of the local air traffic controllers at Cephalton Airport.

He focuses on dealing with threats to the town of Cephalton proper (brain), while she focused outside the town on the Shire (body). They were like two 'adrenaline junkies', enjoying the excitement of both emergencies and their time of intimacy together. Very quickly they fell in love and had a passionate romance.

Of course, there is the other side to Rosie. The same woman, who is all action when necessary, can 'chill out' when she needs to and indeed does so for much of the time. Life is not one long emergency and, like the conservative Reaction side of the family, she often relaxes, shuts out the daily dramas and tries to keep her life as undisturbed and even-keeled as possible. During these quiet times, she eats more, sleeps more and becomes rather sluggish. Indeed, Cephalton, and the Shire as a whole, is a busy, but relatively quiet community, unless Rosie is in action mode. In her quieter more intimate moments, her tears, sighs, breathless delight and beautiful blush of embarrassment, reveal a more tender and very winsome Rosie Reaction.

Rosie is close to Brenda Bridgehead (insula) and her partner Dr Ernie Enkephalin (periaqueductal grey matter). Brenda keeps a general eye on Rosie and, knowing the impact she can have on everyone when aroused, encourages her to take things steadily. If Rosie is in pain, Ernie is quick to act. If she over-reacts, Brenda is quick to calm her down.

Rosie is particularly close to her ever-listening, and utterly devoted Uncle, Tim Tickertaste (solitary nucleus), one of the oldest, and most conservative, members of the Downtown community. She finds it hard to consider life without her rather eccentric uncle, who has always been there for her and dotes upon her.

Meet the Downtown Dream Team

The Dream Team, with the exception of Al Zheimer (who lives in Midtown), live close together in Downtown Cephalton, on the Faceandear and Swallowtalk properties. The team consists of:

Tony Turnon: locus coeruleus – lives on the Faceandear property with connections all over Cephalton. His own property is very small but, because of his critical role throughout Cephalton, his influence is way beyond the size of his property. He is the sometime lover to Rosie Reaction, who in the adrenalin of the moment of a crisis, he saw blush with excitement and never looked back from the pursuit of passion with her.

When Tony turns on the siren of his mobile rescue vehicle the whole town hears it. When Tony is awake, for certain everyone else is awake. He is part of the crack emergency team that is assembled to protect Cephalton during times of threat, natural disaster and crisis. Anyone else would find the occasional excitement of emergencies exhausting enough, but not Tony. He also works as an air traffic controller at Cephalton Airport, a job for which he is particularly well suited given his phenomenal concentration.

Dr Ernie Enkephalin: periaqueductal grey matter – lives by the Sylvian Canal in Downtown Cephalton and is intimately involved with Brenda Bridgehead. He is the town doctor with a special interest in, and clinic for, pain relief. Ernie is a leading authority on the use of opiates and works closely with the anaesthetist and sleep specialist, Dr Raffi Restogen. Together they deal with any emergencies requiring anaesthesia or urgent pain relief.

Dr Raffi Restogen: raphe nuclei – is an anaesthetist living on the Faceandear Estate. He runs a specialist sleep clinic and works closely with Dr Ernie Enkephalin in his pain relief clinic. His ability to induce a state of relaxation, calm and wellbeing is legendary. His beautiful smile and hypnotically large eyes contribute to his popularity and many of the ladies in Cephalton have fallen asleep in his arms. He has a way of uplifting everyone's spirits and reducing tension just by being there.

Tim Tickertaste: nucleus solitarius – he has no partner and lives alone but compensates for this by living in the heart of the Downtown Dream Team community. He is a tall thin man who works with, and lives on, the property of Sam Swallowtalk, the Director of the Cephalton power station. Tim and Sam have a joint obsession: to ensure the efficient working of the power supply to Cephalton and the Shire. Tim is a rather eccentric engineer, who is Rosie's favourite uncle, and in his spare time writes *Cephalton's Good Food Guide.* Of course, the truth is that he has never cooked for himself and eats out at all the restaurants in town. According to their owners he never forgets a bad meal.

Al Zheimer: nucleus of Meynert – one of the great old men in Cephalton, he is really only a nominal member of the Dream Team. He lives on the border of Uptown and Midtown Cephalton between Priscilla's and Uma's places, close to the southernmost parts of Fredrick and Rochelle's Estate, and therefore away from the rest of the Dream Team. He is Chairman of the Board of Directors of the Cephalton Emergency Services. Having made his fortune in the pharmaceutical industry, he bankrolls all of Fredrick's political decisions for major infrastructure in Uptown Cephalton. He also provides donations on a regular basis to the Cephalton Historical Society, run by Sage, whom he so admires that he has made him his sole heir. He also takes a fatherly interest in Fredrick, Rochelle and Annie. Like so many others he is captivated by Rosie. He has always loved Corrie O'Graphie, but knows that her heart is given to Frank Finesse.

While they all have their own individual interests and jobs, the Dream Team maintain the life and activity of the town and Shire, from day to day and in emergencies. Their combined skills are awesome in maintaining crisis alert systems (linked in with Annie Almond and Uma Underbride), dealing with emergencies – from fire-fighting to acute life support – and keeping the information technology and power supply of the whole community online.

They are the ultimate 'network of networkers' – the Dream Team – a small group of people upon whom the whole of Cephalton and the Shire depend. They have connections with everyone in town and have a pervasive, though often invisible, influence on all that happens. During crises, Uma Underbride is their immediate boss and Director of Emergency Services. For the rest of the time, they listen to everyone, from Frank Finesse to Fredrick Foresight, but none more than Rosie Reaction. The Downtown Dream Team love Rosie Reaction and her far-flung family and she loves them. They are all so close that Rosie and her relations and the Downtown Dream Team community blend into each other.

Rosie usually keeps excellent health and most people in Cephalton just take for granted what she does, until she is unwell. When she is ill, she becomes pale, lightheaded, weak, tired and has difficulty thinking clearly. Her vision sometimes becomes blurred and she begins to tremble. She can become suddenly clammy and nauseous, and then collapse with low blood pressure. At other times she becomes hot and flushed with a rapid irregular pulse and her blood pressure can be dangerously high.

Sometimes she can have difficulty passing urine and at other times she is incontinent. She may also become constipated. At her worst, she has no tears when she cries, no sweat when she is overheated and no saliva when she is chewing food. Needless to say, she has difficulty during these times feeling anything of physical desire or sexual excitement with Tony Turnon. When unwell she has little control of all the normal things she can usually take for granted in her daily life. She finds that she cannot rely on her body to cope with change or to get on with her normal work.

Sometimes she experiences episodes of startled, uncontrollable fear and vivid memories of former traumatic experiences in her life. She becomes anxious without any clear reason and can faint at the sight of a needle for taking blood.

When there are problems in the health of members of the Downtown Dream Team, the whole of Cephalton feels less safe.

Tony Turnon is usually all go. But when he is sick he has difficulty focusing and goes from one thing to the other, without purpose or direction. He wakes up during the night in a panic, wide-eyed, staring and heart pounding. He has had to be off work at times when his concentration has not been good enough to ensure the safety of aircraft in his role as an air traffic controller.

Dr Ernie Enkephalin ironically has episodes of severe pain for which the cause has not been obvious. At other times, in the midst of a busy day and clinic, he has failed to realise he has cut himself, as if he feels no pain.

When *Dr Raffi Restogen* is unwell he loses his calm sense of wellbeing, cannot sleep and may become anxious, irritable and depressed.

Tim Tickertaste sometimes has episodes of vomiting, and irregular heart rate and breathing.

Al Zheimer has suffered from memory lapses, inability to take on new information and emotional outbursts for very minor reasons. When he has been at his worst, he does not even know who he is.

The autonomic nervous system and the reticular formation explained

Location and structure

Within the autonomic nervous system (ANS), the sympathetic nervous system (SNS) lies on either side of the spinal cord in the thoracic and lumbar regions and is composed of a collection of ganglia or knots of nerve tissue. The parasympathetic nervous system (PNS) lies within the cranial nerves and in the sacral spinal cord and is also composed of a collection of ganglia.

The reticular formation (RF) forms a central core arising from the spinal cord, concentrating in the brain stem, and ascending to the entire brain and consists of:

1. The periaqueductal grey matter surrounds the aqueduct of Sylvius (Sylvian Canal in Cephalton)

2. The locus coeruleus (pons)

3. The raphe nuclei (pons)

4. The nucleus of Meynert (anterior to hypothalamus)

5. The nucleus solitarius (medulla)

6. The nucleus ambiguous (medulla)

7. The parabrachial nucleus (medulla)

Connections

The ANS receives input from the hypothalamus, the reticular formation and the spinal cord and gives output to the spinal cord and the reticular formation (as part of a feedback loop between the two).

The reticular formation also receives input from the hypothalamus as well as from the cerebellum and the spinal cord. The reticular formation provides diffuse output upwards to subcortical and cortical structures and to the cerebellum as well as downwards to the ANS and spinal cord.

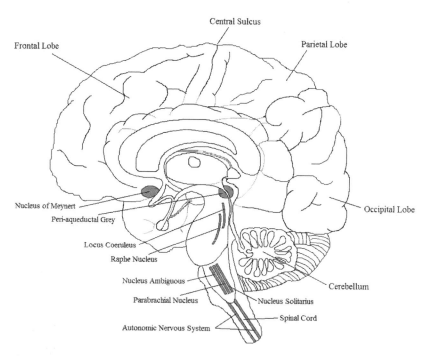

Figure 20.1. Medial view (inner surface) of the right side of the brain showing the reticular formation and the autonomic nervous system, shaded in grey. Each of the main visible lobes of the brain are labelled. Note how many separate structures there are that form these systems.

Functions

The functions of the ANS and RF replicate some of those of the hypothalamus. The difference is that whilst the hypothalamus activates, the

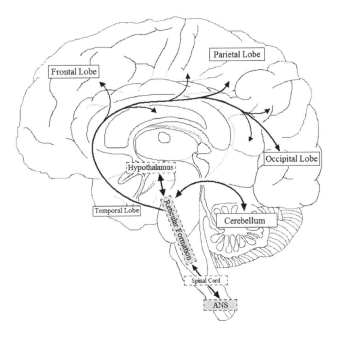

Figure 20.2. Medial view (inner surface) of the right side of the brain showing a schematic representation of the main connections of the autonomic nervous system (ANS) and reticular formation. Note the characteristic feature of the reticular formation is a broad network of connections of many structures.

reticular formation provides expert guidance which the ANS implements. Together, they enable homeostasis to be achieved and ensure normal function and the ability to response to a threat or crisis:

- *Emergency response*: the SNS deals with fright, fight and flight.

- *Conservation response*: the PNS deals with calming, resting and digesting (for fuller detail see Chapter 17).

- *The maintenance of life support and conscious experience*: in addition the RF, through ascending pathways radiating out into the subcortical and cortical areas, regulates mood, memory, pain, blood pressure, pulse, breathing, swallowing and cortical arousal (sleep, wakefulness and attention) – all vital components of life, both conscious and unconscious.

The specialised functions of the RF include:

* Pain regulation (periaqueductal grey matter)

* Alertness (locus coeruleus)

* Mood and sleep (raphe nuclei)

* Arousal and memory (nucleus of Meynert)

* Respiratory and blood pressure regulation (nucleus solitarius)

* Speech and swallowing (nucleus ambiguous)

* Respiratory regulation (parabrachial nucleus)

These last two are not mentioned in the Cephalton story for the sake of brevity. However, like so many parts of the brain, though obscure, they are important.

Technical corner

All communication within the brain occurs through neurotransmitters (see Chapter 1). There are approximately 100 neurotransmitter systems but in this chapter we mention those most relevant to the reticular formation and the ANS. There is often overlap between systems to ensure back-up in the event of system failure.

1. *Serotonin* is produced in the raphe nuclei (Dr Raffi Restogen) and distributed throughout the brain, and especially in the emotional centres (limbic system). It is involved in the regulation of mood and sleep.

2. *Noradrenalin* is produced in the locus coeruleus (Tony Turnon) and distributed throughout the brain, especially in the amygdala and cerebral cortex. It is involved, along with histamine, in the regulation of alertness and emergency responses.

3. *Gamma-aminobutyric acid (GABA)* is produced and distributed all over the brain. It is involved in the regulation of brain activity, generally acting as a brake to overactivity.

4. *Glutamate* is also produced and distributed all over the brain. Like GABA it is involved in the regulation of brain activity, but unlike GABA, it generally acts as an accelerator.

5. *Acetylcholine* is produced in the nucleus of Meynert (Al Zheimer) and is distributed throughout the brain, but especially the hippocampus and basal ganglia. It is involved in movement and memory.

6. *Dopamine* is produced in the basal ganglia (Corrie O'Graphie) and distributed to the nucleus accumbens (Priscilla Prizeman) and the limbic system. It is involved in movement and motivation.

7. *Enkephalin* and other opiates are produced in the periaqueductal grey matter (Dr Ernie Enkephalin) and the insula (Brenda Bridgehead) and distributed to the limbic system and down the spinal cord. It is involved in the relief of pain and distress.

8. *Histamine* is produced in only one place in the brain – the hypothalamus (Uma Underbride) – and only one place in the hypothalamus – the tuberomammillary nucleus. It is distributed throughout the brain. It is involved in the regulation of alertness along with the noradrenalin system.

When things go wrong

Disorders affecting the ANS will usually have an impact upon both the PNS and the SNS. These include vasovagal syncope, sacral neuropathy in diabetes mellitus and familial dysautonomia (Riley–Day syndrome).

1. *Vasovagal syncope.* In vasovagal syncope, a very common and usually non-serious problem, there is overactivity of the PNS, leading to sudden lowering of the blood pressure and subsequent fainting. This can occur because of a threat such as the sight of blood, being in an inescapable situation or becoming overheated.

2. *Sacral neuropathy.* Chronically high glucose levels in diabetes mellutus lead to damage to the sacral component of the PNS, with subsequent bladder and sexual problems, and to the thoracic and lumbar sections of the SNS, with subsequent lowering of blood pressure. This is one of the most serious and invisible complications of diabetes. It is not common in the community as a whole, but is common in those with poorly controlled diabetes.

3. *Familial dysautonomia.* The most common features of this rare disorder are: low blood pressure, due to failure of sympathetic activity; vasodilatation of the skin due to erratic sympathetic activity; lack of tears, dry mouth, urinary retention and impotence, all due to failure of parasympathetic activity.

Disorders affecting the reticular formation are the same as those affecting the pons and medulla and include: stroke, tumour, trauma, infection, and demyelination (for further information see Chapter 18). However, in terms of altered function, consciousness may be impaired as in a delirium, sleep may be impaired as in disorders of initiating and maintaining sleep or even hypersomnia (oversleeping), pain sensation may be dulled or heightened, and memory may be lost or fluctuating.

The characteristic feature of disorders of the reticular formation is that widespread, diffuse effects on components of consciousness can be caused by relatively small areas of dysfunction because of the role of these structures in supporting networks of arousal or inhibition, pain relief or pain.

Rosie Reaction and the Downtown Dream Team in summary

Rosie and the Dream Team play a vital role in the Cephalton community and the Shire beyond. Although Rosie can relax and enjoy life and the members of the Dream Team have their own interests and hobbies, when it comes to an emergency, they are all readily available. They function as a highly efficient, smoothly integrated and coordinated team. Without them disasters would not be averted and life would forever be threatened.

Further reading

Levenson, R.W. (2003) 'Blood, sweat, and fears: the autonomic architecture of emotion.' *Annals of the New York Academy of Sciences 1000*, 348–366.

Low, P.A. and Engstrom, J.W. (2005) 'Disorders of the autonomic nervous system.' In D.L. Kaspar, E. Braunwald, A.S. Fauci, S.L. Hauser, D.L. Longo and J.L. Jameson (Eds) *Harrison's Principles of Internal Medicine*, 16th edition, pp. 2428–2433. New York, NY: McGraw Hill.

Part Five

The Community as a Whole

Chapter 21

Cephalton in Action: the Annual Ball

Once a year the whole community come from all over Cephalton to meet for the Annual Cephalton Community Ball. In fact, preparations go on all year. But everything comes together to make this the gala event in the Cephalton calendar.

The Mayor, Fredrick Foresight (frontal lobes), and his partner, Rochelle Ringbond (cingulate gyrus), have invited everyone to meet on Pleasure Island at one of the huge conference facilities on Felicity Feelall's (thalamus) property. Brenda Bridgehead (insula) has organised the planning meetings, which are chaired by Fredrick or Rochelle, and the minutes are kept and actioned by Dudley Doit (motor cortex).

Brenda's private networking amongst the 'movers and shakers' has been formalised in public announcements released from all the news outlets. The voice of Cherry Chatterley (Broca's area) on televisions and radios all over lets everyone know what is happening and when.

Sage Seahorse (hippocampus) has provided Cherry with excerpts from the Historical Society's archives of great occasions in the past, when the Ball was especially memorable. Christopher Crosstalk (corpus callosum) and Charles Chatterley (Wernicke's area) have connected up the town with huge radio speakers and television screens to provide live coverage to enable all those who cannot get to Pleasure Island to enjoy the night.

Maurice Mapply (parietal lobes) has provided the layout for the Great Ballroom with mathematical precision, with maps everywhere to show where everything is, including toilets, fire exits, drinks stalls and first aid facilities. Brenda and Tim Tickertaste (nucleus solitarius) have chosen the food and drink and Uma Underbride (hypothalamus) has advised on quantity.

Brenda has organised the Cephalton Beauty Queen Pageant and Priscilla Prizeman (nucleus accumbens) will give the awards. Although Fay Faceandear (pons), with her wonderfully expressive smile, and Melissa Mirrorwood (somatosensory cortex), with her considerable attention to her appearance, stand a fair chance of winning, the hot favourite this year, with her ecstatic glow, is Olivia Orgasmia (septal nucleus).

Lilly Listentale (temporal lobes) has organised the music and Penelope Panorama (occipital lobes) the decorations, including a display of photographs from previous Balls, between them providing a truly memorable evening of sound and light. Penelope will, of course, also be the official photographer. Tony Turnon (locus coeruleus) has ensured that the sound and light systems are working well.

There are many other behind-the-scenes activities that make this well-coordinated event such a success. Al Zheimer (nucleus of Meynert) provides funding every year, often anonymously, to make sure there is plenty of everything that is needed. Sam Swallowtalk (medulla) ensures an adequate power supply. Dr Raffi Restogen (Raphe nucleus) and Dr Ernie Enkephalin (periaqueductal grey matter) are on duty to deal with those who are accidentally injured or overcome by the excitement of the occasion.

Rosie Reaction (autonomic nervous system) is relaxing on the night of the Ball, but she and Uma are on standby in case Annie warns of any dangers or threats to public safety. Horace Hormone (pituitary) has his emergency medicines on hand for Ernie and Raffi to use if necessary.

What is Felicity, the hostess, doing during all this activity on her estate? She is busy checking that everyone is feeling okay and giving and receiving feedback on how things are going. The night of the Cephalton

Community Ball is no relaxing time for her, nor for her admirer, Christopher, who is kept busy networking.

But the real action happens when Fredrick gives the go-ahead to Dudley Doit (motor cortex) for the dancing to begin. When everyone takes to the floor it is clear that Corrie O'Graphie (basal ganglia) and Frank Finesse (cerebellum) are the most elegant and beautiful dancers in town. Their dancing is outstanding for its consummate ease and grace, and they provide a model for everyone else. Corrie has taught everyone the dance routines and Frank has gone over every step numerous times to make sure that everyone can move with elegant and effortless precision. The evening is a great occasion, with the coordinated and integrated activity of each member of the community of Cephalton ensuring its success.

This is not to say that things cannot go wrong in Cephalton. This year at the Annual Ball was no exception. Halfway through the evening Fredrick Foresight (frontal lobes) felt rather tired, perhaps due to all the late nights involved in its planning, and he lost his usual decisiveness. Rochelle Ringbond (cingulate gyrus), distracted by this, lost her concentration on the big picture. Dudley Doit (motor cortex), used to being guided by Fredrick and Rochelle, was unsure what to do. Brenda Bridgehead (insula) was disgusted when she realised that Uma Underbride (hypothalamus) had been overeating to the point of vomiting. Cherry Chatterley (Broca's area) tried to rescue the occasion by making an announcement, but her throat was hoarse, her voice would not come out as she wanted and she could not think what to say. She looked to her brother Charles (Wernicke's area), who at that moment was becoming muddled by all the requests being made to him to talk to Cherry and get the evening back on track. Fay Faceandear (pons) had a blank expression on her face, seemingly deaf to what was happening around her.

Tony Turnon (locus coeruleus) was a little the worse for wear having had too much to drink and when he failed to operate the sound and light systems properly, mayhem descended. Maurice Mapply (parietal lobe) got lost in the dark and Frank Finesse (cerebellum), also having drunk too much, staggered around the darkened room, ultimately falling in an ignominious heap. Corrie O'Graphie (basal ganglia), so used to Frank's gracefulness on the dance floor, lost her balance, tried to retain her perfect movements, but eventually lost all her rhythm. Olivia Orgasma (septal nuclei), having become extremely excited by the occasion, was now in a rage at what was happening. Priscilla Prizeman (nucleus accumbens), having earlier been egged on by Olivia, had just succumbed to the effects of various illicit substances. Al Zheimer (nucleus of Meynert), having failed to wake her, tried to drive her home, but could not remember where he had left his car. Brenda gave up trying to get everyone to work together and sat in the corner overcome by emotion. Even Raffi Restogen lost his usual calm and composure and became uncharacteristically moody, upset and irritable. Felicity Feelall (thalamus) was overwhelmed by everyone's discomfort.

Annie Almond (amygdala) told Uma that this was her worst nightmare come true and she must do something. Uma immediately stopped gorging herself and consulted with Rosie Reaction (autonomic nervous system) and the Downtown Dream Team (reticular formation), including the wayward Tony Turnon. Rosie got everyone from the Shire to stop eating and drinking and to focus on getting order back into the occasion. Sam Swallowtalk (medulla) and Tim Tickertaste (nucleus solitarius) restored the power supply and Tony Turnon sobered up and reinstated the light and sound systems. A number of people had been injured staggering around in the dark. Horace Hormone (pituitary) had all the appropriate medications available within minutes and Dr Ernie Enkephalin (periaqueductal grey matter) and Dr Raffi Restogen (raphe nucleus) treated those with pain and injuries as quickly as possible.

Everything eventually settled. Christopher Crosstalk (corpus callosum) and Felicity arranged for simultaneous giant screens to be activated across the Shire and Cherry read a message from Fredrick and Rochelle announcing that the crisis was over and everything was now back to normal. Dudley asked Corrie and Frank to move to the centre of the floor and resume the dancing. Annie remained alert but not alarmed. Brenda re-grouped and, with Uma and Horace, provided a sense of calm that spread throughout the whole community. Rosie and her family relaxed. Tony, a little chastened by his lapse, focused on whatever music and visual displays Lilly Listentale (temporal lobe) and Penelope

Panorama (occipital lobe) wanted for the rest of the evening. Raffi, with his beatific smile and radiating calm, endowed such a sense of wellbeing that deep sleep and sweet dreams were guaranteed for all as they left feeling good at the end of the night.

Sage Seahorse (hippocampus) looked warmly across to the love of his life, Annie, and to his much loved mentor, Al Zheimer. He then strolled across to a quiet spot in the corner of the dance hall, took out a pen and note book from his pocket and wrote, 'The Annual Ball, 2008, for inclusion in *Chronicles of Cephalton and the Shire*'.

Farewell to Cephalton and the Shire

You have now met the Town and Shire,
A Who's Who of lower and higher.
The world within that reveals a world around,
A community in which the self is found.

To feel, to do, to note what's seen,
To hear, to speak, to feel; to mean
That when we look to all that's dear,
We call upon a world so near.

No hypothetical deductive proof,
Can substitute this experienced truth,
Of our collective hopes and fears,
The sum of all our joys and tears.

Now you know this unblemished truth,
That whether we be aged or youth,
Our world is within the fleshy fat
Between our ears and beneath our hat.

Glossary

Acetylcholine: A neurotransmitter found in high concentrations in the basal nucleus of Meynert, the hippocampus, the basal ganglia and throughout the autonomic nervous system.

Acromegaly (gigantism): An excess of growth hormone from the anterior pituitary, often due to hyperpituitarism, leading to excessive growth, very tall stature. The biblical Goliath is thought to have had acromegaly.

Action potentials: Electrical signals that travel down the axon and trigger chemical changes in the axon terminal that result in neurotransmitter release.

Adaptation: A behaviour, development or characteristic that increases the likelihood of survival of self and/or biological relatives.

ADHD: See attention deficit hyperactivity disorder.

Adrenal gland (ad = towards, renal = kidney): The endocrine gland located at the top of each kidney that implements the stress response by the synthesis of cortisol and adrenaline. It helps to regulate blood pressure.

Adrenaline (or epinephrine): A hormone released by the adrenal gland in times of danger to prepare the body's 'fight or flight' response. It is a powerful constrictor of blood vessels. Dentists use it to localise and stop bleeding.

Adrenocorticotropin hormone (ACTH): Secreted by the pituitary to stimulate the adrenal gland to release cortisol.

Agnosia: The inability to recognise objects because of a difficulty interpreting the sensory information.

Akinetic mutism: A rare condition characterised by loss of speech and movement, in the presence of alertness. It is associated with cingulate gyrus dysfunction and dopamine underactivity.

Alzheimer's disease: The most common type of dementia, a degenerative disease in which the brain slowly deteriorates. Memory, emotional control, planning and decision-making are among the first functions to be affected.

Ammon's horn (cornu ammonis): A part of the hippocampus subject to calcification and scarring, known as mesial temporal sclerosis. It is known by the abbreviation CA.

Amotivational syndrome: A syndrome characterised by an enduring loss of initiative, apathy, and lack of persistence or social concern, caused by frontal lobe damage, substance abuse or chronic schizophrenia (negative symptoms) and solvent sniffing.

Amphetamines: A drug of addiction that increases the release of dopamine and noradrenalin from neurons that have synapses in the nucleus accumbens. Some of its effects are similar to cocaine.

Amygdala (Latin for 'almond'): A part of the temporal lobe responsible for emotion, emotional memories and single trial learning.

Aneurism: A local blood-filled bulge of a blood vessel often due to disease or to a weakened wall in the blood vessel.

Anomia (or nominal dysphasia): The inability to find the name for objects, and one of the symptoms of Wernicke's aphasia.

Anorexia nervosa: A disorder characterised by extreme weight loss, morbid fear of weight gain and distorted body image.

Anoxia: A lack of oxygen.

Anterior: Pertaining to the front of the brain, or of the brain region being described.

Anterior cerebral arteries: Major arteries for the frontmost part of the brain.

Anterior cingulate gyrus: The front part of the cingulate gyrus that provides one of the connections between the thinking brain (frontal lobes) and the feeling brain (amygdala, temporal lobe).

Anterior commissure: The anterior part of the corpus callosum.

Anterior fossa (Latin for 'cave'): The large cavernous space at the front of the cranial cavity mostly filled with the frontal lobes.

Anterior motor cortex: See premotor cortex.

Anticonvulsant medication: Used to treat seizures such as those in epilepsy, and as a mood stabiliser in bipolar disorder.

Antidiuretic hormone (vasopressin): Produced by the posterior pituitary to suppress urine production, secreted predominantly during sleep.

Antisocial personality disorder: Characterised by a long-standing history of lack of empathy, warmth, remorse or acceptance of social norms. Such people can commit severe acts of disregard or even injury to someone without feeling any remorse.

Aphasia: See dysphasias.

Apraxia: The inability to do things because of difficulties transforming intentions into actions by the cerebral cortex.

Arcuate fasciculus: A part of the inferior longitudinal fasciculus, linking the frontal lobes with Broca's and Wernicke's area.

Asperger's syndrome: See autistic spectrum disorders.

Attention deficit hyperactivity disorder (ADHD): A disorder occurring in childhood and characterised by overactivity and an inability to concentrate.

Auras (Latin for 'breeze'): An unusual experience, sensation, feeling or perception, occurring just prior to a seizure or migraine, that is in the person's awareness and often in his or her memory afterwards.

Autistic spectrum disorders: A continuum of difficulties in socialisation and communication with a tendency towards rigidity and obsessionality. The severe end is often known as autism and the mild end as high functioning autism or Asperger's syndrome.

Autoimmune disease: The body's immune system develops antibodies that attack the body.

Autonomic nervous system (ANS): The system involved with basic body function such as heart rate, arousal, breathing and hormones.

Axons: Long, narrow, tube-like structures that form part of the 100 billion (10^{10}) neurons in the brain. The axons carry electrical impulses away from the cell body of the neuron to the synapse at the end of the neuron.

Basal ganglia: Collection of nuclei consisting of the caudate, putamen, globus pallidus and substantia nigra. Involved in movement and procedural (skill-based) memory.

Basal nucleus of Meynert: A group of cell nuclei anterior to the hyopthalmus, part of the reticular formation.

Basilar arteries: Major arteries of the brain stem.

Bilateral lesions: Lesions occurring in both the right and left hemispheres.

Blind-sight: Although apparently blind, due to cortical damage, some people have a degree of unconscious 'automatic residual vision'. They can respond relatively accurately to a visual image despite seeming unable to see it.

Brain stem: The part of the brain just above the spinal cord, including pons and medulla, and vital to survival.

Broca's area: Part of the frontal lobe associated with expressive language.

Broca's dysphasia: Damage to Broca's area resulting in difficulties expressing language whilst retaining the ability to understand.

Cannabinoids and cannabis: See tetrahydrocannabinol.

Carotid system: The anterior and middle cerebral arteries.

Caudate nuclei: See basal ganglia.

Central nervous system (CNS): The name given to the brain and spinal cord.

Central pain syndrome: A rare neurological disorder characterised by extreme hypersensitivity to pain, due to damage to the thalamus and a lowering of the pain threshold.

Central sulcus: The large groove that runs across the surface of the brain, the cortex, separating the frontal and parietal lobes and marking the division in the brain between the motor cortex and the sensory cortex.

Cerebellar peduncles: Connections between the cerebellum and the pons and medulla.

Cerebellar syndrome: Dysfunction of cerebellum leading to a drunkenness-like syndrome.

Cerebellum (Latin for 'little brain'): Located at the back of the brain, behind the brain stem and below the occipital lobes, whose main function is fine adjustments to movement.

Cerebral haemorrhage: The rupture of an artery resulting in a bleed in, or around, the brain.

Cerebral palsy: A developmental disorder characterised by increased muscle tone and abnormalities of movement and posture, as a result of cerebral dysfunction.

Cerebrospinal fluid (CSF): Straw-coloured fluid produced and found in the brain's ventricles and the central canal of the spinal cord.

Cerebrovascular accidents (CVAs): A range of problems that can occur in the brain such as gradual blockages (thrombosis), bleeds (haemorrhages) and travelling clots (emboli) due to disruption of blood flow in the cerebral vessels.

Cerebrovascular disease: Diseased arteries in, or connected to, the brain and leading to damage or dysfunction of the brain.

Chromosomal abnormalities: Abnormalities in the number or structure of chromosomes.

Cingulate gyrus (cingula = Latin for 'girdle'): Part of the limbic system and the frontal lobes divided into two parts: the anterior in the frontal lobes and the posterior in the parietal lobes. Main functions include sustained attention, goal-directed behaviour, attachment and emotional processing.

Cocaine: A drug of addiction that increases the stimulation of dopamine and noradrenalin by blocking their re-uptake at the presynaptic neurons in the nucleus accumbens. It was used originally as a method of staunching blood flow because of its ability to close blood vessels and is still used in ophthalmic surgery.

Cognitive inflexibility: The difficulty in shifting attention from one task to another, or from an intrusive or distressing thought.

Complex partial seizures: Mixtures of sensory, motor or psychological components, with or without impairment of consciousness.

Conduct disorder: A disorder, first apparent in childhood, characterised by disregard for social rules/norms and authority and, in some, a precursor to antisocial personality in adulthood.

Conductive dysphasia: Occurs when the arcuate fasciculus between Broca's and Wernicke's area is impaired, resulting in difficulties linking receptive and expressive language.

Contextual memory: Memory for a certain place or situation, located primarily in the hippocampus.

Coprolalia: The semi-involuntary utterance of obscenities seen in about a third of those who suffer from Tourette's syndrome.

Corpus callosum ('The great body'): A very thick bundle of nerve fibres, located above the thalamus and below the cingulate gyrus. It connects the left and right hemispheres of the brain, allowing communication between the two.

Cortex (Latin for 'bark of a tree'): The outside layer of the brain, made up of grey matter.

Cortical arousal: Increased level of neuronal excitability that enables consciousness, concentration and communication.

Corticobulbar: Connections between the thinking brain and the vital centres in the brain stem, including those regulating swallowing, talking and facial movement.

Corticocerebellar: Connections between the thinking brain and the regulator of precision movements.

Corticohypothalamic: Connections between the thinking brain and the regulator of stress.

Corticolimbic: Connections between the thinking brain and the emotional brain.

Corticospinal: Connections between the thinking brain and the neurons that connect to the muscles in the body.

Corticostriatal: Connections between the thinking brain and the movement brain.

Corticothalamic: Connections between the thinking brain and the central relay for sensation from all over the body.

Corticotropin releasing hormone (CRH): Released by the hypothalamus at times of stress, stimulating the pituitary to secrete adrenocorticotropic hormone (ACTH).

Cortisol: A stress hormone released by the adrenal gland during stress, depression and major physical illness.

Cranial nerves: A set of nerves responsible for controlling sensation from and motor information to the head and neck. They arise mainly from the medulla and pons and correspond to the peripheral nerves for the rest of the body.

1 Olfactory nerve for smell.

2 Ophthalmic nerve for vision.

3 Oculomotor nerve for eye movement, pupillary size and focusing.

4 Trochlear nerve for eye movement.

5 Trigeminal nerve for chewing and facial sensations.

6 Abducens nerve for lateral eye movement.

7 Facial nerve for facial movement, taste at the front of tongue, tear production and salivation.

8 Auditory nerve (sometimes called the vestibulocochlear) for hearing and balance.

9 Glossopharyngeal nerve for swallowing, taste at back of tongue and salivation.

10 Vagal nerve for parasympathetic communication to the organs of chest and abdomen and laryngeal movement.

11 Accessory nerve for head and shoulder movement.

12 Hypoglossal nerve for tongue movement.

Declarative memory: Conscious memory.

Deep brain stimulation: The placement of electrodes in the brain, used as a treatment for severe intractable tremor, dystonia and depression.

Déjà vu: The strong feeling or conviction that a current experience has happened previously although it is extremely unlikely to have done so.

Delirium: Fluctuating levels of consciousness leading to a deterioration in attention, focus, perception and cognition, together with emotional disturbance or distress, due to dementia or systemic illness.

Delusion: Fixed false belief.

Dementia: A degenerative illness involving the gradual loss of memory and other brain functions.

Demyelination: The loss of the myelin cover (fatty insulation) around the axon.

Dendrites: The main receiving structures for nerve cells, analogous to the ears receiving auditory information or the eyes receiving visual information.

Dentate gyrus: A part of the hippocampus, and one of the few parts of the brain in which new neurons are produced throughout life (neurogenesis). This process is improved by antidepressants, lithium, exercise and some anticonvulsants and reduced by prolonged stress and depression.

Depression: A disorder characterised by lowering of mood, loss of appetite, energy and drive.

Developmental dyspraxia: See also dyspraxia. A delay or deviation in the development of sensory–motor integration in children, especially common in boys and manifested as clumsiness.

Dexamethasone: An artificial cortisol with about 40 times the potency of cortisol.

Dexamethasone suppression test: A test of the ability of the hypothalamus to turn off the stress response when sufficient cortisol is available.

Dopamine: A neurotransmitter found in high concentrations in the nucleus accumbens and the basal ganglia, involved in such brain functions as movement and motivation.

Dopamine antagonists: Drugs that work to reduce dopamine activity.

Dopamine receptors: Receptors in the brain configured to interact with dopamine.

Dysarthrias: Difficulties with the motor mechanisms of speech.

Dyslexia: Difficulty with reading or comprehension of the written word.

Dysphasias: Difficulty in communication due to a breakdown in the exchange of information between Broca's area, Wernicke's area, the arcuate fasciculus and the insula.

Dyspraxia: The inability to initiate and integrate movement correctly.

Elective mutism: See selective mutism

Embolus: A blood clot, piece of blood-borne fat or air that travels from one place in the body to another, causing a blockage or embolism.

Enkephalin: An opiate neurotransmitter found in high concentrations in the periaqueductal grey matter in the brain stem.

Executive function: Higher levels of cognitive function such as attention, memory, planning, decision-making and goal-directed behaviour.

Extrapyramidal system: Part of the CNS responsible for regulating muscle tone.

Familial dysautonomia: A disorder of the autonomic nervous system affecting the development and survival of sensory, sympathetic and some parasympathetic neurons. Symptoms include insensitivity to pain, inability to produce tears, poor growth, sexual dysfunction and labile blood pressure.

Flaccidity: Sustained decreased muscle tone.

Follicle stimulating hormone (FSH): Released from the anterior pituitary to help promote the growth of follicles in the ovary.

Foramen magnum: The largest opening in the cranium, through which the spinal cord passes. It is the 'great opening' in the occipital bone.

Fourth ventricle: One of the four fluid-filled cavities in the brain, diamond-shaped and located posterior to the pons and upper medulla, beneath the cerebellum.

Frontal lobes: The largest lobe of the brain, situated anterior to the central sulcus and responsible for executive and motor function.

Fusiform gyrus: Located along the ventral (inner) surface of the temporal lobe with strong linkage to the occipital lobes, the somatosensory cortex and thalamus. It has a specialised role in the recognition of faces.

Gamma-aminobutyric acid (GABA): The main inhibitory neurotransmitter found in abundance all over the brain, but especially in the cortex and basal ganglia.

Geometric reasoning: The capacity to think through a problem or a situation with an awareness of space, shape and the relationships between them, and a component of visuospatial skills.

Glial cells (Latin for 'glue'): Cells making up more than half the brain's volume, which envelop neurons to provide mechanical support, nutrition, immunity against infection and waste disposal of dead tissue, and contribute to myelin sheath production.

Global dysphasia: Occurs when there is widespread damage to the speech areas, and all types of dysphasias are present.

Globus pallidus: See basal ganglia.

Glutamate: The main excitatory neurotransmitter found in abundance all over the brain, but especially in the cortex and the basal ganglia.

Gonadotropin releasing hormone: Secreted from the hypothalamus, it stimulates the release of luteinising hormone and follicle stimulating hormone from the pituitary.

Grand-mal seizures: See also seizures. A severe epileptic seizure that involves loss of consciousness and violent convulsions.

Grey matter: The collection of neurons in the brain that have grey colouring due to cell bodies and lack of myelinated (fatty sheath) axons.

Growth hormone (GH): Released by the anterior pituitary and promotes growth, especially in the long bones.

Growth hormone releasing hormone: Secreted from the hypothalamus, it stimulates the release of growth hormone from the pituitary.

Hallucinations: False sensory experiences.

Heroin: A drug of addiction that stimulates opiate receptors in the brain, causing euphoria, pain relief and depression of breathing.

Higher visual association cortex: Forms the anterolateral border of the secondary visual cortex and is responsible for the interpretation of visual stimuli and a vital component of visual memory.

Hippocampus (Latin for 'seahorse'): A part of the temporal lobe whose main functions include new learning, contextual memory, conscious memory and linking of emotions to memory.

Histamine: A neurotransmitter involved, along with the noradrenalin system, in the regulation of alertness.

Homeostasis (Latin for 'standing at the same place'): The maintenance within a certain range of such variables as body temperature, salt or water balance and hormone production.

Homunculus (Latin for 'little man'): 'Maps' found in the somatosensory cortex and the motor cortex that correspond to the body parts they represent in feeling or action, respectively. The scale is based, not on the size of the body part sending the feedback to the somatosensory cortex, or the muscles commanded by the motor cortex, but on the size of the representation in the brain for that part.

Huntington's chorea (also known as Huntington disease): A hereditary degenerative illness characterised by involuntary and irregular movements and progressive mental deterioration.

Hyperpituitarism: Overactivity of the pituitary gland, resulting in excessive growth, hyperthyroidism and excess stress response and sexual development.

Hypertension: Raised blood pressure.

Hyperthyroidism: Overactivity of the thyroid gland with the resultant increased metabolism.

Hypopituitarism: Underactivity of the pituitary gland, resulting in hypothyroidism and decreased growth, stress response and sexual development.

Hypothalamic syndrome: A rare condition involving damage to the hypothalamus, resulting in under- or overactivity of the hypothalamus with effects on appetite, thirst and sleep.

Hypothalamus: Located in the floor of the third ventricle, below the thalamus and above the pituitary, responsible for controlling the endocrine and autonomic nervous system (ANS) and regulating temperature, hormonal activity, salt and water balance. Also provides the emergency responses required for acute threat and stress.

Hypothyroidism: Underactivity of the thyroid with resultant hypometabolism.

Infarctions: Damaged and dead tissue due to a lack of normal blood supply.

Inferior longitudinal fasciculus: A large, long bundle of fibres that connects the occipital lobes with the posterior part of the temporal lobes – the 'what' pathway.

Inferior parietal lobule: The lower part of the parietal lobe that integrates auditory, visual and movement information with spatial awareness.

Inferomedial: Refers to any part of the brain that is the under or lower part and toward the midline of the brain.

Insula: The hidden fifth lobe of the brain lying below the frontal lobes, medial to the temporal and anterior to the parietal lobes, functioning as a bridge connecting many vital structures and functions.

Ischaemia: A localised lack of blood supply often due to a blood clot, blockage or haemorrhage which may result in lack of oxygen – hypoxia.

Jamais vu: The opposite of déjà vu, feeling that something or someone familiar is unfamiliar.

Lateral fissure (Sylvian fissure): A large groove creating the top boundary of the temporal lobe and helping to separate the frontal from the temporal lobe.

Lateral ventricles: The largest two of the brain's four ventricles.

L-Dopa: A medication, actually a neurotransmitter, used in Parkinson's disease to help restore the level of dopamine and norepinephrine in the brain, made famous in the movie *Awakenings*.

Lexicography: The discipline of writing and editing dictionaries, and reflected in the collection and editing process in Wernicke's area.

Limbic system: The emotional brain, including nucleus accumbens, amygdala, hippocampus, cingulate and hypothalamus.

Locus coeruleus: Located in the pons, above and to the sides of the periaqueductal grey matter, the only major source of noradrenalin axons for the brain cortex.

Lower motor neuron lesion: A breakdown between the primary motor cortex and the voluntary muscles due to a problem occurring outside the brain or spinal cord, which leads to long-term flaccidity.

Lower visual association cortex: A part of the secondary visual cortex that forms the bulk and central core and is responsible for the gathering and integration of information about visual stimuli.

Lutenising hormone (LH): Released from the anterior pituitary to act on the ovaries to release an ovum.

Macropsia: Seeing things as larger than they actually are.

Magnetic resonance imaging (MRI): A brain imaging technique that uses the magnetic properties of organic tissue to gain images of the brain.

Marijuana: A drug of addiction that has an indirect effect of increasing dopamine in the nucleus accumbens, and a direct effect on receptors, called cannabinoid receptors, which mimic the effects of schizophrenia.

Medulla: A part of the brain stem below the pons and above the spinal cord, and like the pons, involved in maintaining basic functions such as heart rate and breathing.

Meninges: The three layers of membranes and thick coverings surrounding the brain and spinal cord.

Meningitis: Inflammation of the meninges.

Mesial temporal sclerosis: See Ammon's horn.

Mesocortical dopamine pathway: A mental activity and memory pathway for dopamine that connects the nucleus accumbens with the cingulate gyrus and frontal lobes. Disruption of this pathway leading to under-activity can result in negative symptoms of schizophrenia.

Mesolimbic dopamine pathway: A mood and memory pathway for dopamine that connects the nucleus accumbens with the amygdala and hippocampus. Overactivity of this pathway can result in the positive symptoms of schizophrenia.

Methamphetamine: A stimulant drug used for elevation of mood and the induction of a chemical dissociative state.

Methylphenidate: A stimulant medication used in the treatment of ADHD.

Micropsia: Seeing things as smaller than they actually are.

Middle cerebral arteries: Major arteries for the middle part of the brain, especially those areas involved in speech and movement.

Middle fossa (Latin for 'cave'): The large cavernous space at the back and top of the cranial cavity largely filled with the sensory part of the brain including the parietal, temporal and occipital lobes.

Middle temporal gyrus: A gyrus of the temporal lobe, located between the superior temporal gyrus and inferior temporal gyrus, whose main function is to make sense of sound and contains a large part of the secondary auditory or association cortex.

Migraine: A type of severe headache, generally throbbing, that can result in alterations in blood flowing through different parts of the brain. These alterations can cause symptoms such as severe headaches and visual hallucinations.

Mixed dysphasia: Occurs when both Broca's and Wernicke's area (and their surrounds) are damaged, resulting in a mixture of receptive and expressive language problems.

Moebius syndrome: A rare developmental condition in which there is a failure of the facial nerve to stimulate muscles in the face and characterised by the inability to smile, suck and speak clearly.

Monoamines: A specific subtype of neurotransmitters; for example, serotonin and dopamine.

Motor cortex: The part of the frontal lobes responsible for planning and initiating movement. Divided into primary and secondary (premotor).

Motor neuron: Those neurons involved in motor activity.

Motor neuron disease: Progressive neuronal degenerative disorders that destroy motor neurons.

Multiple sclerosis (MS): A chronic, inflammatory and progressive degenerative disease that attacks the myelin axons in the central nervous system.

Muscle tone: The sustained, automatic contraction of muscles that helps to maintain posture.

Myelin: Insulating material of a fatty substance (phospholipids and proteins) that covers most axons.

Narcolepsy: A disorder characterised by frequent episodes of falling asleep associated with a defect in the arousal system.

Negative symptoms of schizophrenia: The reduction or loss of usual behaviours leading to, for example, poverty of thought, poverty of emotional expression, loss of motivation and decision-making, loss of planning, and poor hygiene.

Neologism: A made up word.

Neoplasms: Abnormal cell production.

Nerve fibres: See axons.

Neurodegenerative diseases: Diseases where there is gradual deterioration of the function and structure of the brain.

Neurogenesis: The production of new neurons, stimulated by exercise, antidepressants, lithium and some anticonvulsants but impaired by stress and depression.

Neuroglial cells: See glial cells.

Neurons: Cells in the brain that receive from and transmit information to other neurons via electrochemical impulses. There are approximately 100 billion (10^{11}) of these in the adult brain.

Neuropathy: A disease process in the nerves, usually referred to in relation to the long nerves outside the central nervous system (peripheral nerves).

Neurotransmitter: A naturally occurring chemical in the brain that transmits the signal between neurons at synapses or exchange points between neurons.

Night terrors (pavor nocturnus): A sleep disturbance characterised by manifestations of panic but differentiated from nightmares in that the sufferer cannot easily be woken and has no memory of it.

Nigrostriatal dopamine pathway: A movement and memory pathway for dopamine that connects the nucleus accumbens with the caudate nucleus, putamen and substantia nigra. Too little dopamine in this pathway produces increased muscle tone known as dystonia and Parkinsonism.

Noradrenalin (also norepinephrine): A type of neurotransmitter – a catecholamine – which is the precursor for dopamine and is associated with stress.

Nucleus accumbens: A subcortical structure, located beneath and to the back of the frontal lobes, involved in reward.

Nucleus ambiguous: The motor nucleus in the medulla responsible for the control of speech and swallowing.

Nucleus basalis of Meynert: Part of the reticular formation, and a major source of acetylcholine.

Nucleus of solitary tract (nucleus solitarius): Located in the brain stem and involved with taste and the regulation of cardiac function.

Obsessive compulsive disorder (OCD): Experience of obsessions (disturbing and intrusive thoughts of a forbidden or threatening nature) and compulsions in an attempt to relieve anxiety.

Occipital lobe: The smallest of the four lobes, located at the back of the brain, behind the parietal lobes and above the cerebellum. Responsible for integrating and disseminating visual information.

Optic chiasm: Where the optic nerves cross from one hemisphere to the other.

Optic tracts: The bundles of axons that travel from the retina to the visual cortex.

Orbitofrontal lobes: The lowest part of the frontal lobe above the bones that hold the eyes (the orbits).

Oxytocin (Greek for 'rapid birth'): Released from the posterior pituitary to stimulate contraction of the uterus during birth, also associated with a sense of wellbeing.

Panic attacks: A sudden onset of intense fear, often without any obvious trigger. Due to overactivity of the sympathetic nervous system.

Parabrachial nucleus: The motor nucleus responsible for respiratory regulation.

Paraesthesiae: Sensations such as pain, tingling, crawling beneath the skin (formication), without any obvious stimulus.

Parasympathetic nervous system (PNS): See autonomic nervous system. Attempts to settle emergency responses by the body's organs.

Parietal lobe: One of the cortical lobes of the brain that sits behind the frontal lobe, above the insula and temporal lobe and in front of the occipital lobe. Functions include awareness and analysis of the environment, attention and arithmetical processing.

Parkinson's disease: A degenerative disorder of those parts of the brain (basal ganglia) involved with movement and tone and characterised by tremor, slowness of movement and thought, and loss of emotional expressiveness in face and voice.

Partial seizures (simple): Seizures that occur in the absence of impairment of consciousness or convulsions, and manifested by a sensory, motor or psychological experience such as aura.

Partial seizures (complex): Similar to simple partial seizures but with involvement of more than one unusual experience, a psychological component or impairment of consciousness.

Periaqueductal grey matter: The grey matter located in the brain stem that contains opiate receptors and releases enkephalin, one of the brain's natural painkillers.

Perinatal hypoxia: A reduction of oxygen in the baby's blood supply around the period of childbirth.

Petrous temporal bones: The bones that sit immediately beneath and lateral to the temporal lobes. The word petrous simply means stony or rocky.

Phantom limb: The phenomenon of experiencing sensation or pain in a limb that has been previously amputated, believed to be a persistent cortical representation of the absent limb.

Phenylalanine: An amino acid that can be converted to the neuro-transmitters, dopamine and noradrenalin.

Phenylketonuria: A disorder in which the enzyme necessary to break down the amino acid phenylalanine is absent with a potential for brain damage in the absence of the correct diet.

Pituitary: The major endocrine gland located at the base of the hypo-thalamus, which secretes hormones into the general circulation, regulating growth, stress, metabolism and reproduction.

Pons (Latin for bridge): Located in the brain stem and involved in basic functions such as sleep, waking, hearing, balance and pain control. It is the bridge between the cerebral hemispheres and the cerebellum.

Position emission tomography (PET): A brain scan that measures metabolic activity in the brain.

Positive symptoms of schizophrenia: Unusual behaviours, thoughts and perceptions, such as hallucinations, delusions, increased arousal and the behaviours that arise from them.

Posterior: Pertaining to the back of the brain, or of the brain region being described.

Posterior cerebral artery: Major arteries for the back of the brain.

Posterior cingulate gyrus: The back part of the cingulate gyrus that connects the thinking brain (frontal lobes) and the perceptual brain (parietal lobes).

Posterior commissure (splenium): The back and smallest part of the corpus callosum.

Posterior fossa (Latin for 'cave'): The large cavernous space at the back and bottom of the cranial cavity largely filled with the brain stem (midbrain, pons, medulla) and the cerebellum.

Posterior inferior cerebellar artery syndrome (PICA): Damage to this artery leads to loss of sensation down one side of the body, paralysis of the palate (difficulty swallowing) and vocal cords (difficulty speaking) and loss of balance (ataxia).

Post-synaptic neuron: The neuron that is positioned after a synapse and in receipt of information from receptors (which act like ears for each neuron).

Post-traumatic stress disorder (PTSD): An intense and persisting response to trauma characterised by high levels of anxiety, arousal, flashbacks of the event and determined avoidance of any reminder of the event.

Prefrontal cortex: The anterior part of the frontal lobe involved in all aspects of planning and working memory.

Premotor cortex: Also called secondary motor cortex, anterior to the primary motor cortex. The premotor cortex helps to plan and prepare for movement and forwards information to the primary motor cortex.

Primary motor cortex: That part of the motor cortex located at the posterior part of the frontal lobes, responsible for initiating movement.

Procedural memory: A memory for a procedure or sequence of actions such as typing, riding a bike or playing a musical instrument, the main centres for which are in the basal ganglia.

Prolactin: Released from the anterior pituitary to stimulate the production of breast milk (lactation), inhibits ovulation to some degree and reduces male libido.

Prosopagnosia: The inability to recognise and identify faces due to damage to the fusiform gyrus, part of the temporal lobes.

Purkinje cells: Cells in the cerebellum that are particularly susceptible to oxygen loss because they are high consumers of oxygen. Damage to these cells can result in jerky movement of the eyes known as nystagmus, staccato-like movements and ataxia.

Putamen: See basal ganglia.

Pyramidal pathways: General motor pathways emanating from the motor cortex and travelling down the spinal cord. So called because of the shape of the motor pathways as they cross over in the medulla.

Raphe nuclei: See reticular formation.

Reticular formation: Originates in the brain stem and extends upwards into the brain and down into the spinal cord. It contains many nuclei, including the raphe nuclei, locus coeruleus, basal nucleus of Meynert, solitary nucleus and the periaqueductal grey matter. The reticular formation is mainly involved with sleep, waking, alertness and pain.

Rubella virus: Responsible for 'German measles', with infection in the first 16 weeks of pregnancy leading to the possibility of deafness and brain, cardiac and eye abnormalities.

Schizophrenia: A psychiatric illness in which a person experiences symptoms such as thought disorder, difficulty expressing emotions, delusions and/or hallucinations.

Secondary auditory cortex: That part of the temporal lobe in which sound is interpreted before being integrated with other sensory modalities, such as vision.

Secondary motor cortex: See premotor cortex.

Seizures: Unusual electrical impulses in the brain characterised by abnormal thoughts, emotions, behaviour, sensations, motor activity and, in the case of many types of epilepsy, loss of consciousness.

Selective attention: The capacity to attend to a particular task or aspect of the environment.

Selective mutism (also called elective mutism): Avoidance of speech in specific situations probably due to intense social anxiety.

Sella turcica (Turkish saddle): The saddle-shaped part of the sphenoid bone in which the pituitary is situated.

Sensory–motor integration: Information exchange between the somatosensory cortex and the motor cortex.

Septal nuclei: Part of the nucleus accumbens and involved with pleasure states such as orgasm and rage.

Serotonin (also known as 5-hydroxytryptamine or 5-HT): A neurotransmitter involved with mood regulation and anxiety.

Set shifting (shifting attention): The ability to flexibly switch attention between stimuli, themes or tasks.

Somatosensory cortex: Anterior part of the parietal lobe providing awareness of body and body image and containing the sensory homunculus.

Spasticity: Sustained, extreme, increased muscle contraction and tone.

Spatial disorientation: Inability to work out location and direction.

Sphenoid bone (butterfly-like): This is situated at the junction between the anterior and middle cranial fossa with extensions on each side, shaped like wings.

Spinal cord: The part of the CNS located within the spinal column.

Split brain: Severing of the corpus callosum to prevent epilepsy in one hemisphere spreading to the other.

Staccato movements: Movements that lack smooth transition from one part of the movement to the next, giving a jerky or robotic quality.

Stimulant medication: Medication used in the treatment of ADHD, for example methylphenidate and dexamphetamine, which enhance dopamine activity.

Stroke (see Cerebrovascular accidents)

Stroop task: A neuropsychological test assessing the ability to shift mental set or cognitive flexibility.

Subcortex: Brain region below the cortex or outer layer of the brain, which is largely made up of white matter.

Substantia nigra: See basal ganglia.

Superior longitudinal fasciculus: A large, long bundle of fibres that connects the superior frontal lobe with the top parts of the parietal and occipital lobes (sometimes referred to as the 'where' pathway).

Supervisory attentional system (SAS): A psychological model, describing how the brain's response can be flexible in line with current goals, available cognitive resources and unfamiliar situations. See also cingulate gyrus.

Sylvian fissure: See lateral fissure.

Sympathetic system: See autonomic nervous system.

Synaesthesia: The experience of two sensory experiences being blended such as a person seeing sounds or feeling colours.

Synapse: The space and meeting place between two neurons which allows communication between neurons.

Temporal lobe: Located alongside the frontal and parietal lobes and anterior to the occipital lobes, responsible for receiving, integrating and disseminating auditory information.

Temporal lobe epilepsy: See complex partial seizures.

Tentorium cerebelli (Latin for 'tent of the little brain'): A thick, brown, canvas-like covering that limits the movement of the brain and torsion of the brain stem. It separates the middle from the posterior cranial fossa and sits above the cerebellum and below the occipital lobes.

Tetrahydrocannabinol (THC): One of the key active ingredients in cannabis that acts on receptors in the brain for similar, endogenously produced, substances called cannabinoids. If overstimulated these receptors produce a schizophrenia-like syndrome.

Thalamus (Latin for 'bridal' or 'pleasure chamber'): The major sensory relay station and regulator of pain threshold.

Third ventricle: One of four connected fluid-filled cavities within the brain and surrounding the thalamus.

Thought disorder: A common feature of schizophrenia, in which thoughts are difficult to follow and understand, because each component fails to connect conceptually to others.

Thyroid stimulating hormone (TSH): Released by the pituitary, stimulates the thyroid to produce thyroxine.

Tourette's syndrome: A developmental disorder characterised by rapid, involuntary muscle contractions (tics), affecting mostly the face, neck, vocal cords and limbs, and frequently associated with obsessive compulsive disorder. It is believed to be due to overactivity of the dopaminergic systems of the basal ganglia.

Transient global amnesia: Complete memory loss for a discrete period of time, usually but not always due to vascular (blood vessel) causes.

Tuberoinfundibular pathways: One of the major dopamine pathways involved in prolactin regulation, with both the hypothalamus and pituitary being involved.

Uncinate fasciculus: A bundle of fibres that connects the orbitofrontal cortex with the front part of the temporal lobes (uncus). This connection enables communication between the amygdala and the frontal lobe, between affect and cognition, feeling and thinking.

Uncus: See uncinate fasciculus.

258 / Who's Who of the Brain

Upper motor neuron lesion: A breakdown between the primary motor cortex and the voluntary muscles due to a problem within the brain or spinal cord, which leads to a long-term increase in muscle tone.

Vasovagal syncope: The most common type of fainting (syncope) when the parasympathetic system leads to low blood pressure and decreased cortical arousal.

Ventral tegmentum: A midbrain structure located close to the nucleus accumbens and the major source of dopamine for the front of the brain.

Ventricular system: A set of structures within the brain that produce and contain the fluid that flows around and in the brain and spinal cord – the cerebrospinal fluid. It provides a rapid chemical communication system, maintains brain shape and protects from the impact of trauma.

Ventromedial: Extending to both the ventral surface (the under surface of the brain) and the midline (medial).

Vermis (Latin for 'worm'): The central part of the cerebellum where the two halves or hemispheres meet.

Vertebral column: The collection of smaller bones, stacked on one another, that form the spine.

Vertebral system: One of the two main arterial systems supplying the back and base of the brain.

Vertebrobasilar insufficiency: Diminution of blood supply to the cerebellum and brain stem, which affects balance and coordination. If prolonged, vital functions such as heart and respiration can be affected.

Visceral memories: Memories that trigger a bodily or 'gut reaction' and are associated with nausea or vomiting, involving especially the insula.

Visual agnosia: The inability to recognise a visual image even though it is actually part of the person's experience, often resulting from damage to the secondary visual cortex.

Visuospatial skills: The skills necessary for visuospatial memory and the ability to distinguish, process and integrate spaces, shapes and patterns in the environment.

Visual cortex: Located in the occipital lobe and divided into primary (receiving visual information from the eye) and secondary (in which visual information is processed and interpreted).

Voluntary muscles (skeletal muscles): These are involved with movement and posture and under direct control from the motor cortex.

Wernicke's area: A brain region involved with communication, specifically the reception of language.

Wernicke's dysphasia: Damage to Wernicke's area resulting in difficulties understanding speech.

White matter: Brain matter that is made up of billions of axons, given a white colour by their surrounding fatty myelin.

The Authors

Kenneth Nunn

Paediatric Neuropsychiatrist, University of New South Wales; Emeritus Consultant at the Children's Hospital Westmead and Senior Staff Specialist, Justice Health New South Wales.

Tanya Hanstock

Doctor of Clinical and Health Psychology and Senior Clinical Psychologist at The Bipolar Program, Hunter New England Area Health Service, Newcastle, Australia; Academic Conjoint Lecturer with The School of Psychology at the University of Newcastle and the University of New England, Australia.

Bryan Lask

Emeritus Professor of Child and Adolescent Psychiatry, St George's University of London, UK; Medical Adviser, Huntercombe Hospitals, UK; Visiting Professor, University of Oslo; Research Director, Regional Eating Disorders Service, Ulleval Universitetssykehus, Oslo, Norway.

Illustrations

Linn Iril Hjelseth was born in 1981 and grew up in the north of Norway. She has been drawing her whole life, and people are her great interest. She studied art and film for two years, and then psychology for a year before comleting a BA in Visual Art and Design. She had her first solo exhibition in summer 2007.

Edward Clayton

Doctor Edward Clayton is a Livestock Research Officer at NSW Department of Primary Industries, Wagga Wagga Agricultural Research Institute and Adjunt Senior Lecturer with the Charles Stuart University in the EH Graham Centre for Agricultural Innovation, Australia.

The brain diagrams in this book are by Edward Clayton, Tanya Hanstock and Kenneth Nunn.

INDEX

Made in the USA
Lexington, KY
17 January 2014